# COPING WITH

# An Illiterate

# Parent

# COPING
## WITH

# An Illiterate

# Parent

CESAR CHAVEZ HIGH SCHOOL
8501 Howard
Houston, Texas 77017

## Nancy N. Rue

ROSEN PUBLISHING GROUP, INC./NEW YORK

Published in 1990 by The Rosen Publishing Group, Inc.
29 East 21st Street, New York, NY 10010

*First Edition*

Library of Congress Cataloging-in-Publication Data

Rue, Nancy N.
    Coping with an illiterate parent.
    Includes bibliographical references.
    Summary: Advice for young people whose parents can't
read in helping to deal with what is really a whole-
family problem and changing that situation for the better.
    1. Literacy—United States—Juvenile literature.
2. Reading (Adult education)—United States—Juvenile
literature.   3. Teenagers—United States—Family relation-
ships—Juvenile literature.   [1. Literacy.   2. Reading
(Adult education)]   I. Title.
LC151.R84   1990   306.874   89-10756
ISBN 0-8239-1070-9

# ABOUT THE AUTHOR ◇

**N**ancy Rue spent her first twenty-five years in the East. Born in New Jersey, she was raised in Florida, educated at Stetson University, DeLand, Florida (B.A., English) and the College of William and Mary, Williamsburg, Virginia (M.A., Education), and baptized by fire into a teaching career at Booker T. Washington High School in Norfolk, Virginia.

With her husband, Jim, she moved in 1978 to Nevada, where her daughter Marijean was born and where she taught for six years before "retiring" to free-lance writing. From the time she was ten, consuming two Nancy Drew books a day, she had thought she could write the sort of things kids could love. Now it was time to find out if she were right. With Fang, her computer, she has put out six books and more than fifty short stories, articles, and plays. Although awards have come her way (*Campus Life* Award of Merit and Outstanding Book of the Year award of the Books for Young Adults Program), she most treasures letters from readers who have consumed Nancy *Rue* books.

Along the way she and her husband became involved professionally in the theatre and together founded Nevada Children's Theatre. Their goal is to provide high-quality theatrical experiences for audiences of—you guessed it—young people.

# Contents

# COPING WITH

# An Illiterate

# Parent

# CHAPTER 1

# Mark's Story

**W**hen Mark was a little boy he didn't know that his father couldn't read. In fact, it never occurred to him to think about it one way or the other. To him, reading was something adults just did—like worrying and driving and yelling at their kids.

Like most little guys, Mark figured his dad could do anything: at 6'5", tipping the scales at 200-plus, he could work two jobs—one in construction and one as a security guard—build the coolest swing sets and jungle gyms in the neighborhood for Mark and his sister Debbie, fix anything that broke—tricycles to pick-up trucks—and keep their family safe from bogeymen and burglars and imaginary alligators that lived under the bed. He was Dad. Mark looked up to him, obeyed him, maybe even feared him a little. He sure never considered whether or not he could read.

Hindsight, of course, is the sharpest kind of vision. Looking back now, Mark remembers that his father never read to him when he was little. That was his mother's job. His father didn't hunker down over the bills, or look at the mail, or even look at his report card. All of those were Mom's duties, too. Mom took care of everything that involved words on a page—shopping lists, birthday cards, complicated-looking forms and applications. Even when the family went out to eat in a restaurant, his mother read the entire menu out loud before anyone ordered, a tradition Mark always thought was for his and Debbie's benefit. His father never read a newspaper, consulted *TV Guide*, nor offered to help him with his homework, and yet none of it ever struck Mark as strange. Dads couldn't do that stuff because they were either out making a living, or they were sitting in their chair resting from being out making a living.

But Mark was suddenly shoved out of his innocence and into a shocking realization when two things happened to him almost simultaneously.

The first: He turned into an adolescent. It was natural that at age twelve he should realize that his once all-knowing father was not infallible and start looking at him with a more critical eye. Like every other kid in junior high, he began to discover that his father dressed like a dweeb, listened to nerdy music, and talked like somebody out of the Dark Ages. But Mark's close scrutiny also revealed that his father didn't speak as well as the other dads in their respectable, middle-class neighborhood. Nor did he read the sports pages, keep up with world affairs, or get into home computers. There was something different about his father—something that Mark slowly began to be ashamed of. His dad, it seemed to him, just wasn't as smart as everybody else's dad.

The second occurrence: About six months into

that period of Mark's life his mother was in a serious automobile accident. After several days on the critical list she pulled through, but it was going to be a while, the doctors said, before she would be able to come home and resume her normal duties as Mom. In traction in a convalescent home, she definitely couldn't write notes to teachers, help with homework, handle the grocery shopping, and deal with the electric bill. Suddenly everything fell on Dad.

Perhaps "crashed" is a better word. Mark was aware that the mail was piling up unopened in its basket by the front door and that when his father wasn't bringing home pizza or bags of burgers, he was buying off-the-wall soups or burning TV dinners. Once Mark awoke late at night and sensed that his father was still up. He crept to the kitchen door and peered in, to see his father sitting at the table staring at an insurance form and looking dangerously close to tears. A kind of anxiety he'd never felt before took hold in Mark's stomach. Somehow Dad wasn't keeping them safe from everything the way he always had.

The situation was hardest on Mark's nine-year-old sister Debbie. Mark had always been a strong student, but school was a struggle every step of the way for Deb. She pulled Bs and an occasional A, but only because their mother sat with her every night walking her through spelling words and reading workbooks and social studies puzzles. With Mom tucked away in traction and Dad working until he dropped trying to keep it all together, Debbie wasn't getting any help at home, and, afraid to bother anyone, she wasn't asking for any. Inevitably her schoolwork started to slip, and a note from her teacher came home. Mark saw Debbie hand it to their dad, but he didn't open it right away, and Mark waited all evening for the explosion. After all, teacher didn't send notes home to tell your parents you were being an angel in school. However, nothing happened. Debbie went to bed, and Mark thought his father did, too.

But when Mark went out to the kitchen for a snack late in the evening his father was at the table again, staring at the note. This time, he *was* crying.

Mark had never seen tears in his father's eyes, and he wasn't sure what to do. If it was so bad that Dad broke down over it, it was definitely something Mark didn't want to know about. Close to panic, he turned to bolt out of the room, but his father called to him.

"Son," he said. "I need you to read this for me." As his father wiped his face with the back of his hand, Mark slowly sank into a chair and picked up the note from Debbie's teacher.

"Dear Mr.—" he began, and then stopped. "Why, Dad?" he said.

His father stared hard at the table. Mark had never seen him look that way before. He wasn't strong now. He wasn't tough. He wasn't all-knowing. He was shaken and frightened—and ashamed. It was a look Mark would never forget.

"I need you to read it," his father said finally, "because I can't."

Chances are that Mark never would have found out his father was a nonreader if his mother hadn't been hospitalized. His father had arranged his life so neatly and become so clever at hiding it that only his wife knew. But Mark *had* found out, and at first it was devastating. Man, his dad was *dumb*. If he'd had to go into Debbie's fourth-grade class and take a test, he'd have *flunked*. How did you deal with knowing that about your own father?

Mark was suddenly bent on making sure that none of his friends discovered it. He started making excuses for not inviting them over the way he always had. What if somebody handed his dad one of those typed jokes that were going around? What if somebody asked him if he'd read that article about the Forty-Niners in *Sports Illustrated*? What if somehow it just slipped out?

It also seemed important to keep his father away from school. He conveniently forgot to tell him about open house and worked harder than ever to keep his own grades up so there would be no reason for his father to have any contact with his teachers.

In fact, to be with his father in public anywhere became agony for Mark. Stores were potential scenes for humiliation. He was convinced that everyone was going to stop in the aisles to stare at the thirty-five-year-old man who couldn't read the soup cans. When the three of them went out for fast food, Mark always insisted they go through the drive-in for fear that if they went inside his father would gape open-mouthed at the menu posted on the wall and ask Mark to read it aloud. Even at the convalescent home when they went to visit his mother, he wondered when his father was going to go in the wrong restroom or push a door when it said to pull—and in the process blow the lid off the whole shameful secret.

Mark's reaction did a number on his relationship with his dad. He withdrew from his father as far as he could, limiting his contact to saying hi, goodbye, and good-night. His father actually seemed relieved that Mark didn't want to talk about it further and took to his own corner. It was lonely, but somehow it seemed safer.

Until the night Mark found his father in the kitchen again late at night, this time with Debbie. Mark woke up hearing his sister's voice droning on and, used to having to help look after her, went out to the kitchen to tell her to get out of the refrigerator and into bed. She was at the table with her father, the basket of mail between them. Dad was slitting each envelope open and handing its contents to his nine-year-old daughter, who was slowly, painfully attempting to read it aloud.

"If pay- payment has al - ready been made-" She stopped and gave a huge sigh. "Please dis- dis - re—I don't know that word, Daddy."

Growing up is usually a gradual process, but there are sometimes moments when maturity takes an instant, giant spurt. This was one of those moments for Mark. For some unknown reason his father had never learned to read. Maybe he wasn't too smart. Maybe—whatever. But what mattered now was that he needed help, and Mark was the only one who could give it to him without his having to admit his problem to somebody else—and having to get that awful look on his face again. Mark stepped forward and took the letter from Debbie's hand.

In the sixteen months that followed before Mark's mother was allowed to come home, a burden situated itself on Mark's shoulders. Every day after school he helped Debbie with her homework. Then every night he sat at the kitchen table and read the mail to his father. Some nights while his father dictated, he filled out insurance forms, drafted letters to creditors, and made shopping lists. Every Saturday morning he went with his father to the grocery store and translated the list into real food (making sure they got normal soups like chicken noodle instead of the previous beef consommé that his father had guessed to be okay), and every evening at supper time he read the directions on the packages out loud while his father painstakingly followed them at the stove. "I'm sure glad you learned how to cook, Daddy," Debbie told him.

Through it all Mark found out more than he really wanted to know about his parents' finances and the awesome responsibility of keeping a family going, and at first he resented it. He was thirteen, and he was doing his father's job for him so they wouldn't end up starving or filing bankruptcy. At thirteen, in his opinion, he should have been kicking back, munching pretzels, and watching MTV, totally ignorant of the fact that it was such a drag to be an adult. It wasn't fair. Why had his father never bothered to learn to read when he was a kid?

One night when he'd already spent two hours doing his own homework and was an hour into trying to decipher a letter from his parents' lawyer about the lawsuit they were filing against the driver who had injured his mother, Mark got mad enough to ask him. He wasn't disrespectful—you didn't pull smart ass on Mark's oxlike father. But the resentment and contempt were seething just beneath the surface.

His father, however, seemed to see it as a legitimate question. "I'll be damned if I know, son," he said. "But I look at Debbie and I see the same thing would be happening to her if your mother—and now you—weren't there to help her. Maybe if I'd had a mother who saw I had problems and sat down with me every night, I wouldn't have to be bothering you with this now."

Guilt welled up in Mark's throat. "Aw—you're not bothering me, Dad," he lied.

But his father shook his head, and a look Mark did know took shape on his face—a look of determination and courage and strength. "I'll tell you one thing, though, son," he said. "As soon as your mother is on her feet again, I'm going to go back to school, and I'm going to learn to read. I figure the hardest part is admitting you got the problem and that it's messing up your life. If I can admit it to you, I guess I can admit it to anybody."

Mark felt like the heel of a Reebok. But when his father put out his hand, Mark took it and shook it with everything he had.

Mark, of course, is not his real name, and a few of the details in the story have been changed so that "Mark" and his family won't be recognizable. But in every other way Mark's situation is real, and so are the hurt and the shame and the resentment and the problems that go with it. If you've bothered to pick up this book and read this far, chances are you've felt some of those things yourself. Maybe you're the son or daughter of one of the 25 million adults in America who can't read a note from their child's teacher, decipher directions on an aspirin bottle, or address a letter. Maybe you're the offspring of one of the 35 million who can't understand a daily newspaper, follow a job manual, or manage in today's technological society.[1] Maybe you have a mother

---

[1] Claire Safran, "Illiteracy: Read All About It." *Woman's Day*, October, 1986, p.86.

or a father who, by those standards, is considered illiterate. Perhaps you aren't sure whether that's the case in your family. Illiteracy is considered by our society to be a shameful thing—certainly not something that is volunteered in the course of a casual conversation. "My son's doing great in school, which is amazing, Harriet, because I can't read past the first-grade level myself," is not something you're likely to hear your mother rattle off to a friend over the phone. If your mom or dad has never owned up to having reading problems, it's because he or she has learned to keep the secret well hidden. If they tell people they can't read, they're likely to lose jobs, friendships, even the respect of their own kids.

Again, if you've bothered to pick up this book and read this far you probably have your suspicions. If you see several of the following signs in your parent, it's more than likely that that person has at least enough problems with reading and writing to keep him or her from coping successfully in an increasingly complex society. Your parent:

- Doesn't have reading materials around the house—books, newspapers, magazines.
- Has never (or at least seldom) since you've known him/her darkened the door of a library or bookstore.
- Clicks channels with a remote instead of consulting a television guide.
- Avoids using paper and pencil—doesn't make shopping lists or write letters or take down phone messages. In cases where writing is a necessity, gets a "death grip" on the pen and shows obvious frustration.

- When writing is done, shows practically illegible penmanship.
- Didn't read to you as a kid, or stopped early on.
- Finds reasons not to help you with homework.
- Avoids contact with your school and your teachers.
- When asked to read or spell something, vaguely sidesteps it by saying, "I don't have my glasses with me," or "I'm not sure."
- When reading can't be escaped, reads silently with lips moving and finger following the words, again accompanied by obvious frustration and anxiety.
- Works in a job that doesn't require a lot of reading and writing.
- Doesn't go up for promotions or talk about higher career goals.
- Changes jobs often.
- Is shy, withdrawn, or guarded around strangers.
- Perhaps has a closed mind—doesn't want to discuss new ideas—and is somewhat hostile concerning authority figures ("cops," IRS people, bank officials, bosses).
- Isn't wild about traveling any great distance from home.
- Never tries anything new in a restaurant; orders the same thing no matter what.
- Doesn't try new things period—doesn't get out there and enjoy life!

According to Jonathan Kozol, leading advocate for America's nonreading adults, a person is literate if he has the competence to read and write and comprehend at a level that conforms to his real needs in society.[2] If that definition doesn't fit your mom or dad—if he or she is trapped in a nowhere job, imprisoned by a sense of inferiority, shamed by the inability to give you everything you need intellectually and socially and emotionally because he or she can't read and write competently—then literacy is a problem.

So what does that have to do with you?

A problem with literacy is a family problem. One third of all jobholders are denied advancement because of reading deficiencies.[3] An illiterate adult (by the definition used above) earns 42 percent less than an adult who is literate.[4] Adults without adequate literacy skills have an unemployment rate four times that of those who possess them.[5] That reflects on the family.

With all of that operating against him, coupled with the sense that he or she can't do something every other adult seems to do with ease, a parent with a reading problem has a pretty low level of self-esteem. That can translate into depression, abuse of alcohol and drugs, dysfunction in the family. All of that is bound of reflect on you, too.

So there you are, growing up in a house where people can't live up to their potential because the

[2] Jonathan Kozol, *Prisoners of Silence*, New York: Continuum Publishing Corporation, 1980. pp.55–56.
[3] Carl B. Smith and Leo C. Fay, *Getting People to Read*. New York: Delacorte Press, 1973, p.2.
[4] Jerry O. Nielsen, "Societal Consequences of Adult Illiteracy," in *Teaching Reading to Older Students*, Donald Bear, ed. Reno: University of Nevada, 1989, p.45.
[5] *Ibid.*

skills aren't there. You can either bank on the faint
possibility that when you're eighteen you'll be out
of there and everything will be cool. Or you can do
something about it now. You can, in a way, save
your parent's life and at the same time save a part of
your own, too.

If you want to do that, if you're willing to do that,
this book is for you. It will attempt to do the following
for you:

- Help you think through how your parent's
  problem with literacy is affecting your life.
- Help you see the day-to-day anxieties and
  frustrations your parent faces in not being
  able to read and write adequately.
- Answer your questions with facts and statistics and thus ease some of the resentment and
  confusion you may feel.
- Guide you in steering your parents toward
  the right kind of professional help and in
  giving them some assistance yourself.
- Give you suggestions for coping with the
  problem at home.
- If you're interested, tell you how you can take
  part in the national drive to conquer illiteracy
  in our country.

If you're the son or daughter of a non-English
speaker, this book may be helpful to you, too. Thirty-
seven percent of the adults living in America who
are considered illiterate do not speak English, and
22 percent speak only Spanish.[6] Many of the prob-

---

[6] Lissa Lin, "Illiteracy in America." *Seventeen*, Vol. 47, April, 1988,
p. 98.

lems of living with a foreign-born parent are different from those of sharing a house with an English speaker who can't read, but many of the difficulties are the same. You will want to consult other sources for help with the cultural toughies, but when it comes to coping with the language barrier, much of what you'll find here may help move you in the right direction.

Illiteracy carries a real stigma. If one or both of your parents doesn't read well, ten to one you feel a sense of shame. It isn't your fault—nor is it theirs. But the fact that neither of you is to blame doesn't mean that you as a family can't do something to change it. You're taking the first step right now by turning the page and reading on.

# CHAPTER 2

# "My Dad Can't Read"

**P**at's father read on a second-grade level. He worked as a trucker, which meant days on end away from home and very little time to do anything but work and sleep.

Her mother read about as well as the average fifth-grader. She worked a twelve-hour shift in a casino, which meant night after night away from the house and very little time to do anything but work, sleep, and dole out the household chores to her four kids.

Nobody in the house read for pleasure. Nobody worried about whether there was a quiet place for Pat and her brother and sisters to do their homework. Her parents didn't own an encyclopedia, take the newspaper, or subscribe to any magazines. There wasn't the money to take family vacations, eat out in restaurants, or go to plays or concerts. There wasn't the time to go to the library, write letters, or take up hobbies. There wasn't the motivation to keep a diary, borrow books from friends, or even pick up a magazine at the doctor's office.

When Pat graduated from high school, which she accomplished by running errands for teachers, arranging cheat signals with friends, and staying out of trouble, she read on a first-grade level. She couldn't read a menu, write a check, or find a strange address by looking at street signs. The only job she could get was as a picker-packer in a factory, and she only managed that by taking the application home and having a friend fill it out for her. When she got to work the first day she didn't know whether to push the door or pull it to open it. The word "pull" was printed in bold letters, but she couldn't read it. In fact, she didn't even see it. It took her a long time to make friends on the job because she felt stupid around other people. She was convinced that everybody around her knew she couldn't read, and that made it tough for her to look any of them in the eye or get into a conversation. She'd blow it. She knew she'd blow it. So she just listened.

Not every teenager who grows up in a family with only marginal literacy skills turns out like Pat. If that were true, some of you wouldn't even be able to read this book! But every young person whose parent or parents have a literacy problem is affected in some way—be it academically, socially, emotionally, or even materially. The purpose of this chapter is to put some of the possible effects in front of you and to urge you to take a close look at your own personal situation to see which apply to you. Why do it? Because it's hard to take steps to do something about a problem if you aren't first entirely sure that it *is* a problem. Once you're aware of the influence of illiteracy on you, you may be motivated to take steps to do something about it.

## ACADEMIC EFFECTS

In its April 1983 report, the National Commission on Excellence in Education addressed this statement to parents: "Your child's ideas about education and its significance begin with you. You must be a living example of what you expect your child to honor and to emulate."[1]

If your father's own education was somehow fouled up when he was a kid, how can he do that? How can he, as the report goes on to suggest:

- participate in your education?
- monitor your study?
- encourage good study habits?
- be an active participant in the work of the schools?
- be a model for continued learning?

No matter how much he loves you or how devoted he is to you, if he isn't more than marginally literate, he can't do those things—and as a result *your* education gets fouled up.

The children of poor readers are defrauded in three ways, says Jonathan Kozol, author of *Illiterate America* and *Prisoners of Silence*. The first is that they themselves may have trouble learning to read. In some cases learning disabilities, such as dyslexia (which we'll discuss in more detail later), are in-

[1] Quoted by Jonathan Kozol, *Illiterate America*, (New York: Doubleday, 1985), p.59.

herited. More often, though, children of nonreaders can learn to read (recognize words) in the early grades, but by fourth and fifth grade, when they have to read to learn, they have a hard time because they have no background. They haven't been read to at home. They don't pick up magazines and unconsciously practice comprehension. Reading is not a part of their life, so learning to do it is a lot like learning to speak Russian when no one else around you speaks it.

Second, children of poor readers get the short end of the stick because their parents can't analyze the problems of the schools and help to correct them. Most parents who don't read, speak, or write well are reluctant to go anywhere near the school for fear of being "found out" and embarrassing you as well as themselves. You don't see them at PTA and school board meetings, and you sure don't see them writing letters to the editor or perhaps even reading the bulletins that come home from school with their kids. They may be completely cut off from what's going on in education in their community and so don't exercise their right to speak out on what happens to you in the classroom. Do they want sex education in your school? Do they know a particular teacher isn't doing his job? Do they agree with the new zoning laws that are going to move you halfway across town to another school? They may have very good answers to those questions, but without the proper skills they may be afraid or unable to do anything about them—and so you suffer.

Third, without a strong basis of literacy, even if parents see the warning signs of failure in their kids they may not be able to propose corrective measures in a way that wins attention. When Pat's oldest son, Timothy, started first grade, Pat gathered up every ounce of courage she had and went to his teacher and said, "You're going to have to make sure Timothy knows what he's supposed to do and really help him, because I can't. I can't read." Not every parent has that kind of guts. In fact, most don't, and you can't blame them. Even if they see the signs of their own old problems in school showing up in you, it might be so painful to admit that to a well-educated teacher or guidance counselor that they'd rather endure a root canal—without novocaine. Your parents know you better than anyone. They could probably shed some very valuable light on any learning difficulty you might have. But if they don't feel they can hold their heads up in the same room with someone who has a college degree, they may just have to let you flounder. You can't blame them, but you sure take the consequences.

## SOCIAL EFFECTS

According to Claire Safran, researcher in the area of literacy, the majority of the 35 million Americans who can't read well enough to manage in society today are not bag ladies and boat people, but ordinary folks.[2] In Columbus, Ohio, there's a thirty-year-old exterminator who can't understand the warning labels on the poisons he uses. In Hartford, Connecticut, a forty-five-year-old business executive takes his paperwork home for his wife to read to him. In South Carolina a mother says to her teenage daughter, "Please write this letter for me. You have

[2] Claire Safran, "Illiteracy: Read All About It." *Woman's Day*, October 1, 1986, p.87.

such nice handwriting." Many of the adults with literacy problems are upstanding people just like your parents, and they belie the commonly held belief that all "illiterates" are skid row bums or Mexican mothers on welfare.

However, their weaknesses in reading and writing do affect them—and you—socially.

As mentioned in Chapter 1, one third of all jobholders are denied promotions because they have reading deficiencies. As a result, the illiterate adult generally earns less than an adult who is literate and experiences less satisfaction on the job. Adults without adequate literacy skills have an unemployment rate four times that of those who have them. "A large proportion of illiterates," say the authors of *Jump Start* (The Final Report of the Project on Adult Literacy, January, 1989), "are ordinary working-class Americans who disguise their lack of basic skills by remaining in dead-end jobs with little prospect of improving their lot."[3]

The job a person holds does affect his or her social standing, and your parents' social standing directly affects yours. True, where you live, what label is on your clothes, and what kind of car you drive to school (if you have one to drive at all!) shouldn't determine what kind of person other people think you are—but it's a fact of life that it does have an influence on the kinds of people you attract and the friends you make. It may even affect how you feel about yourself in your teen years. More important, it may affect how you feel about your parents, right

[3] Forrest P. Chisman, *Jump Start: Final Report of the Project on Adult Literacy.* Southport Institute of Policy Analysis, January 1989, p.1.

or wrong. "We're not as good as everybody else because we live in a mobile home and drive a clunky car," isn't a valid statement, but it pops into your head and colors your feelings nevertheless.

And then there's the cover-up. Many young people who know their mom or dad can't read will go out of their way, as Mark did, to conceal that fact from their friends. That's bound to be reflected in their social life. They don't invite friends over. They don't give parties. Some don't even give out their phone number. "Hey, I'll call you, okay?" is better than, "Don't leave a message with my dad. He can't write it down." If you haven't been there you may have the urge to say, "Oh, for Pete's sake! What's the big deal?" But if you've lived in fear that one of your friends in the National Honor Society will discover that your old man can't even read the directions for loading a camera, it makes a lot of sense.

Kids of non-English-speaking parents may have additional problems. When Carla came to the United States from Mexico she was six and the only Spanish-speaking child in her school. If she wanted to communicate with the other children she had to learn their language fast, and she did. Her parents, however, learned neither to speak it nor to read it, largely because they couldn't read or write in their own language. Carla believes that their inability to read English and thus know how things are done here cramped her style big time in high school.

"In old Mexico, where they grew up, if you had a boyfriend you didn't go out—he just came to the house and visited with you while your parents hung around. Guys here aren't going to do that! I couldn't stay out late. I couldn't date.

I couldn't even spend the night at a friend's house. If somebody gave a slumber party, I'd go for an hour or two and then make up an excuse for why my father was coming to pick me up. I didn't expect my parents to be anybody except who they were, but I didn't ever try to explain who they were to my American friends. I just lied a lot and felt a lot of resentment."

Adults with low literacy skills are frequently transient. Opportunities for promotion often require taking a written test. If an employee with inadequate reading skills takes the exam, she may score so poorly that she is demoted or fired; or she may be too frightened to take it at all and quit instead. The job change that results may also involve a move to another area, and that means uprooting the family— perhaps for the umpteenth time. If you've ever had to go through the doors of a school where you knew no one and perhaps have even go through a semester afraid to form any attachments because chances were you'd be moving on again before report cards even came out, you know what that does to your social life, not to mention your academic progress.

## EFFECTS ON FAMILY RELATIONSHIPS

If your parents' literacy problems are common knowledge in your household, you may be called on to do or help do what your parents can't do for themselves—a burden that can stir up resentment like silt from the bottom of a pond. "From the time I was about ten," says Carla, "I was doing things a grown-up would normally handle. I went with my father to buy a car and had to act as translator and fill out all the forms. I mean, he was depending on me, a little girl, to get him a good deal! Now I'm nineteen and have a job and my own life, and they still want me to take the car to the mechanic and go with them to buy a hamburger. I've been so busy living their life I haven't had a chance to live mine!"

For the offspring of English-speaking parents with reading problems, the burden of filling in the gaps may not be so severe. After all, it's possible to survive, to manage, if you can read on a fourth-grade level, and millions of adults are doing it. But little annoyances can creep in and crack a parent-teen relationship that is naturally fragile enough already.

Mark hated having to do his own homework, and then help his sister with hers, and then sit down and help his father with the family bills.

Nancy resented having to write all her mother's business letters for her when, after a day of school and band practice and a part-time job, she was exhausted.

Marianne got so mad she could spit because her father couldn't fill out her financial aid application forms for college. She had to dig through piles of paperwork looking for the right documents before she could even start. It took hours, and through every one she was silently cursing the man who was sitting in the living room watching TV while she pored over stuff she knew nothing about.

There are some things even a maturing teenager can't do for himself—like writing excuses for absences from school or plowing through a tough literature class. If he or she is lucky some other adult who can assist will be available, and there's nothing wrong with that. In fact, it's healthy for a person your age to form other adult attachments. But if a parent feels guilty because somebody else is taking up the slack for him in the kid-raising department, and the kid feels resentful because she has to go elsewhere to get the help she needs, a rift can form pretty quickly.

## EFFECTS ON YOUR SELF-IMAGE

Teachers who work with adults learning to read have seen serious difficulties in their families. They frequently come across folks with drug and alcohol problems, with kids they can't manage, and with histories of divorce that make Liz Taylor look monogamous. These teachers see a direct correlation between the nonreaders' frustration with themselves because they can't do anything to change their station in life and the serious problems that are disrupting their families. If you're a teenager growing up in that atmosphere, with parents who don't feel good about themselves, it's going to be pretty hard for you to form a strong picture of yourself. Isn't this bound to be my lot in life, too? you may ask yourself. "Children of illiterates," writes Jonathan Kozol, "tend to fit themselves into the slots provided for them."[4] A feeling of powerlessness can easily creep in and take up residence in your view of the future.

Pat says not being able to read "puts you in a box." The family that lives with a literacy problem is in a big box together. Exposure to family reading times, to happily poring over brochures and atlases

[4] Kozol, p.76.

planning a vacation, to trips to libraries and museums and obscure events mentioned on the back page of the newspaper—that's all limited. It's often replaced with overworked, underpaid, exhausted, self-doubting parents who pass on a pair of glasses through which you can see only the same kind of life for yourself. Even if you've learned to read well and have gotten yourself a decent education and are determined to make it in this world, you're handicapped by holes in your background. You can do it, but it's going to be harder for you. The fact that there is a literacy problem in your family is a factor you have to reckon with.

# CHAPTER 3

# From the
# Parent's Side

"**G**oing out into the world as an adult and not being able to read—it's like being swallowed by quicksand."[1]

"My one desire is to pick up a magazine in a doctor's office and read like everyone else there."[2]

"Donny wanted me to read to him. I told Donny: 'I can't read.' He said: 'Mommy, you sit down. I'll read it to you.' I tried it one day, reading from the pictures. Donny looked at me. He said, 'Mommy, that's not right.' He's only five. Oh, it matters. You better *believe* it matters!"[3]

---

[1] Susan Hampshire, *Susan's Story*. New York: St. Martin's Press, 1982, p.148.

[2] Michael Clarke, quoted by Louise Clarke in *Can't Read, Can't Write, Can't Talk Too Good Either*. New York: Walker & Company, 1973, p.183.

[3] Quoted by Jonathan Kozol in *Illiterate America*. New York: Doubleday, 1985, p.7.

"I look at my seventeen-year-old son and my twelve-year-old daughter and I want to help them with their homework, but I can't. My son was supposed to repeat the ninth grade for the third time this year.... He finally said he wanted to drop out.... I see my handicap being passed on to my son.... I tell you, it scares me."[4]

Those are real people talking—real adults who suffer because somewhere along the line somebody failed them. Their learning problems, physical or emotional, were not discovered and dealt with, and now they can't live up to their real potential because they can't read well enough to keep up with today's society. After reading Chapter 2, in which we talked about the effects of your parents' literacy problems on you, you might be tempted to go to them and say, "My life's a mess because you can't read. Do something about it!" This is a good place to give you a glimpse of how *they* feel before you make that mistake.

I should warn you first that putting yourself in their shoes is not easy. The authors of *Getting People to Read* put it this way:

The ability to read competently is not automatic, even though most of us take it for granted. For most of us it is a naturally acquired ability so central to all of our other pursuits as to be almost a sixth sense. So easily did we acquire the skill and habit that most of us cannot really remember how and when we learned to read.

[4] *Ibid.*, p.57.

Nor can we imagine how alien and hostile the world seems to those who cannot read at even the survival level.[5]

The closest you may be able to come to putting yourself in their place is following Jonathan Kozol's suggestion: Imagine yourself in the Soviet Union, where even the letters themselves are strange. You can't read the street signs, the buses, the hotel marquees. You can't decipher menus, labels on cans, or even the prices. You're lost and starving, but you're ashamed to ask for help. That, many nonreaders will tell you, is what it feels like to be illiterate.[6]

Contrary to the way the old late movies portray them, people with reading problems are not simple, unlettered, but happy human beings.[7] Your parents are not Annie from *Annie Get Your Gun* or Joe from *Great Expectations*. They are people who face a world where their lack of ability to read well may govern the kind of work they do and certainly governs the quality of life they lead.[8] That makes them neither happy nor uncomplicated. In fact, if you were to ask them and they were to answer unashamedly and honestly, they'd probably make statements like the ones below. They were made by adults with reading problems, adults who are trying to raise kids as well as cope with everything else the world demands. A look into those statements— which may very well be on the tip of your mom's or

[5] Carl B., Smith and Leo C. Fay, *Getting People to Read*. New York: Delacorte Press, 1973, p.3.

[6] Kozol, p.11.

[7] *Ibid.*

[8] Smith, p.107.

dad's tongue—may help you understand their situation a little better.

## "THERE'S NO WAY OUT."

*Trapped, frustrated, helpless* are words frequently heard to cross the lips of adults with literacy problems. Most realize that learning to read would help tremendously, but some have been so devastated by years of being considered slow and unable to grasp things that they're convinced they couldn't learn now if they tried. Others think they might be able to benefit from taking classes, but where do you find classes? Is there time to go to school when you're working ten hours a day just to get by and coming home to two kids and a never-ending pile of laundry and bills? And if you do start going to school, isn't everybody going to know? What if your boss finds out that you couldn't read all this time you've been working for her? The risks and complications stack up in their minds until they can't even see around them.

Some people do try to get help and become even more discouraged. Bob attended a six-week program provided by the state unemployment office, a requirement for collecting unemployment benefits. An untrained volunteer teacher was trying to help thirty people, ages 18 to 82, to improve their reading skills. Everyone was at a different place in reading development. When after taking a pretest Bob found out that 98 percent of the class could read better than he could, his eyes glazed over and he was back to biding his time until the six weeks were over, just as he'd always done in school.

Pat, too, tried a reading class—at a community college. Most of the people in the class could read at a fourth-grade level going in. Pat was down at first grade. The teacher was willing to help, but in front of all those other adults, even though they weren't much more literate than she was, it was unbearable. She went home crying after several sessions and finally quit in frustration.

When people feel so entrapped in their situation, they often experience much the same kind of personal breakdown and defeat that drug addicts and alcoholics undergo. For them it isn't an, "Oh, that's too bad," problem. It's scary.

## "I'M JUST LIVING ON THE MARGIN OF LIFE."

*Limited, marginal, isolated* are other frequently heard words in the vocabulary of a poor reader. In the career world not being able to read and write well obviously cuts down to practically nothing chances of advancing, earning more money, and finding job satisfaction. "Although a literate man or woman is by no means certain of a decent and rewarding job in our society," writes Jonathan Kozol in *Prisoners of Silence*, "it is probably true that an illiterate man or woman has almost no chance at all."[9]

But it isn't only in the job market that that feeling of living on the periphery creeps in. The list of things a nonreader or poor reader cannot do *with pleasure* is almost endless:

- Vote intelligently.
- Serve efficiently on a jury.

[9] Jonathan Kozol, *Prisoners of Silence*. New York: Continuum Publishing Corporation, 1980, p.13.

- Try new recipes.
- Plan vacations.
- Scope out consumer magazines for good buys and products.
- If he or she is religious, read or study the Bible or other writings of the faith.
- Write letters, or read them when they come in the mail.
- Pick out greeting cards.
- Keep a journal.

The list becomes really heartbreaking when it comes to their kids:

- "I can't read the poems my little boy has started writing for me."
- "My ninth-grader got a letter of commendation from the principal, and I don't even know what it says."
- "For the first time since she turned thirteen my teenage daughter wanted to share something with me. She wanted me to read what somebody wrote in her yearbook—and I couldn't make it out."

The little things can be the heartbreakers. Sure, your mom or dad is probably *managing* just fine. But those little things may be keeping him or her from really *living* life to the fullest. It's no fun watching other people do it from around the edges. You've got to get in there and be part of it. Not being able to read makes the chances of that minimal.

## "I FEEL LIKE A FAKE."

It's important to most adults who don't read well that nobody find out. *Embarrassment, shame, humiliation*—those are the words attached to having a secret like illiteracy discovered. Most people who can't read well feel that their condition is synonymous with stupidity, and nobody wants to be seen as stupid. The possibility of ridicule makes the fear of disclosure a pretty big one, which is probably why illiteracy has been called the "hidden handicap".[10] That's also why those who suffer from it become so adept at camouflaging their disability.

"When I got my first job, I had somebody write out all the possible questions that were going to be on the application, with the answers, and I took that with me to the interview."

"At home I'd sit on the couch and pretend I was reading a book so my hushand and kids wouldn't know."

"When somebody at work asked me how to spell something, I'd say, 'I'm not sure. You'd better look it up.'"

"They'd send me into the storage room to get a particular brand of nail, but I couldn't read the codes so I'd say I couldn't find it. Then somebody would show me, I'd memorize where it was, and the next time I'd go right to it."

---

[10] Terilyn Turner, "Using the Computer for Adult Literacy Instruction," in *Teaching Reading to Older Students*, Donald Bear, ed. Reno: University of Nevada, 1989, p.129.

"I hang around with intelligent people and copy the way they talk."

"If we go into a restaurant I order the chicken-fried steak no matter what because I know it's going to be on the menu."

"If somebody hands me one of those typed jokes to read, I tell them I don't have my glasses with me. Hell—I don't even wear glasses!"

"You just have to be careful not to get into situations where it could leak out," says one man who reads on a third-grade level. "But sometimes it can't be helped. Then you fake it. Somebody gives you something to read, you make believe you read it. Somebody starts talking about something that's been in all the papers, you try to act like you know all about it even if you don't. And all the time, you feel totally backward and out of place."

Imagine yourself with some kind of awful secret. Then imagine what it would be like to live in terror of the moment when that secret will be exposed. Wouldn't you get pretty good at lying low? Watching out for traps? Evading? Obviating? Wouldn't you make it your business to set up an arsenal of self-protecting mechanisms? And wouldn't you hate every minute of it?

## "I'M SO DEPENDENT."

Many situations occur in the life of a person with poor reading skills that require him to depend on someone else. Seeking help isn't a shameful thing in itself, but in situations where the average adult can do for himself it can be humiliating. Words like *servitude* and *dependence* start to creep into the thinking. This shouldn't be hard for you to identify with. It's a lot like being sixteen and still having your mother dress you or your father spoon-feed you or your younger brother pick out your friends. Those are things you ought to be able to do for yourself at sixteen, and even though there's someone there to help you, it doesn't do much for your self-esteem. You feel inferior. You feel as if you're being patronized. You feel angry. Pretty soon you start wondering what these people are thinking of you. You become distrustful—not just of them but of everybody—and resentful, too—and let's throw in depressed and withdrawn while we're at it. If you always have to rely on someone else to assist you in the simplest of tasks, that does something to your head.

## "I JUST CAN'T LEARN."

As we'll see in the next chapter, an adult who can't read is seldom to blame for it. Something went wrong somewhere that wasn't his or her fault.

But after years—and years, and years!—of hearing things like, "You're just lazy!" "When are you going to learn?" "He's just slow and he's always going to have problems,"—of perhaps being treated like an imbecile or an incorrigible—of maybe being neglected or punished, it's natural for her to feel that she is responsible and that she never can learn even if she tries—so why try?

Unfortunately, only about 2 percent of the adults with reading problems in America have enough confidence in themselves to think they can make a difference their own lives and respond to reading programs. The experience of the rest has been so filled with failure—they have such negative views of themselves as learners—that it's extremely difficult to rekindle any hope in them.[11] In a vicious circle, they continue to avoid learning.

## "IT'S NO BIG DEAL."

One way to handle any problem is to minimize its importance. Many adults with literacy handicaps will tell you that they're doing just fine. That they never liked reading anyway and don't think they're missing anything. That they can find out everything they want to know from watching TV or listening to the radio. That they'd rather work with their hands than their minds. That they'd rather be happy as they are than be some stuffy intellectual egghead. That reading and writing have nothing to do with their job and family problems.

They're lying.

## "HEY, MY ATTITUDE IS—"

"Screw it! I'm never going to be any better off than I am right now anyway."

"I know what I think. I don't need to read a bunch of other people's opinions."

"Look, I have all the friends I need. I don't need to meet a bunch of strangers."

"Every lawyer (college professor, doctor, researcher—or any other well-educated, successful person) you meet is a crook. They're just out there grubbing for money like everyone else."

---

[11] Kozol, *Prisoners of Silence*, p.5.

"Hey, don't push me. I have all I can do just to function. I don't need to be learning anything new."

What has happened to folks with literacy problems who cop those kinds of attitudes is that they're simply paying a price for not being able to read. They've become hopeless, apathetic, or closed-minded; alienated or hostile or passive in the face of life circumstances that they feel powerless to control; withdrawn, shy, emotionally disabled, or trapped in a life-style of day-to-day economic survival.[12] Whipping out those hackneyed sentences is their way of protecting themselves against having to say, "I don't have the skills to really, truly be happy with myself and with my life." Ask yourself: Could you look people in the eye and say that—or would you cop an attitude, too?

That's a brief look at the feelings often experienced by adults with reading difficulties. Perhaps it has opened your eyes or softened your heart enough to want to help. The next step is to equip yourself with as many facts as possible. The next chapter will assist you in doing that.

[12] Edward V. Jones, *Reading Instruction for the Adult Illiterate*. Chicago: American Library Association, 1981, p.27.

# CHAPTER 4

# The Facts About
# Illiteracy

**W**hen Mark's mother came back from the convalescent home and things began to settle into a new state of normalcy, his father kept his promise to learn to read, and he asked Mark to help. By then, Mark understood enough about how his father's reading problem was affecting him, his dad, and his whole family to want to give him a hand.

He started with the phone book and in the Yellow Pages found Project Literacy. Once a phone number was in front of him, his father showed sudden signs of reconsidering the whole idea, so Mark called for him. The people at Project Literacy were great to both of them, assuring his father that he was neither stupid nor alone and that he'd made a courageous move in even having Mark pick up the phone. Then they gave them a brochure for Mark to go over with his dad. It was stuffed with the answers to the questions that had been bugging Mark ever since he'd found out about his father's problem. Things like:

Is he really considered an "illiterate" even though he can read a little?
Is he some kind of weirdo, or is this common?
Are there a lot of respectable, middle-class adults who can't fill out an application?
Why did it happen? He isn't stupid, so why didn't he ever learn to read?

Armed with the answers to those questions, feeling that he had some facts in his ammunition belt, Mark understood even better what had happened (and hadn't happened!) to his father and was more anxious than ever to help him. Once they got started, he was grateful for the information. It was amazing—and infuriating—how many mistaken ideas people had about adult poor readers, ideas that could have stopped his father right in his tracks if both he and Mark hadn't known better.

Like Mark, you need the facts, so here they are, presented as answers to questions that more than likely have been nudging at the edges of your thinking.

## WHAT IS ILLITERACY ANYWAY?

Actually, there is no standard definition, so it's sometimes quite hard to distinguish between a literate person and an illiterate one. Literacy isn't a single skill. In 1981, UNESCO attempted to define a literate person as one who can read and write a short, simple statement about his/her everyday life,[1] but that proved to be an ineffective way to measure literacy. Nor is it a grade level, to which the National Health Survey tried to limit it by saying that literacy meant having a reading ability comparable to that of the average schoolchild entering grade four.[2] In a two-year study done in Kentucky with adult students registering for adult basic education, researcher Sharon Darling found that the median grade completed in school was grade eight, but the median reading level was grade two.[3] Literacy is more a set of skills that people have in varying degrees. If you think that makes literacy sound rather elusive and hard to pin down, you're right![4]

In the first place, there are two kinds of literacy. *Reading achievement* is the literacy learned in school. Can you read and comprehend a piece of literature? Answer questions about what you've read? Interpret it? Restate it? Apply it to other situations? *Functional literacy* is the application of reading skills to practical tasks, such as looking up numbers in a phone book, filling out a loan application, or writing a complaint letter about your electric bill. When you combine those two, then, you come up with a big, rambly definition of literacy that sounds something like this:

[1] National Advisory Council on Adult Education, *Illiteracy in America*. Washington, D.C.: U.S. Govenment Printing Office, p.1.
[2] *Ibid.*
[3] *Ibid.*
[4] Lawrence Stedmen and Carl Kaestle, "Literacy and Reading Performance in the United States from 1880 to the Present," in *Teaching Reading to Older Students*, Donald Bear, ed. Reno: University of Nevada, 1989, p.10.

*Literacy:* using printed and written information to function in society, to achieve one's goals, to develop one's knowledge, and to reach one's potential.[5]

According to the National Assessment of Educational Progress, which in 1986 came up with that definition, literacy isn't just a matter of decoding (that's educational jargon for "reading"!) and comprehending. Literacy has to do with periodicals (newspapers and magazines), forms, tables, charts, indexes, menus, checkbooks, and advertisements. So they break it down even further into *prose literacy* (reading books, newspaper articles, etc.), *document literacy* (dealing with applications, forms, instructions, etc.), and *quantitative literacy* (any kind of reading involving numbers, such as writing a check, reading prices at the store, adding up the total when making a catalog order, etc.). Some people can do some but not all of those things. Are they "literate" or not?

The closest anyone has come to making sense out of all of that is Jonathan Kozol, who in *Prisoners of Silence* says, "A person is literate if he has the competence to read and write and comprehend at a level which conforms to his *real needs* in society."[6] That means varying degrees for different people in some areas and yet implies certain standards for all. Doesn't every adult need to be able to handle his

[5] Irwin S. Kirsch and Ann Jungeblut, *Literacy: Profiles of America's Young Adults.* Princeton: Educational Testing Service, 1986, p.3.
[6] Jonathan Kozol, *Prisoners of Silence.* (New York: Continuum Publishing Corporation, 1980, pp.55–56.

legal affairs, deal with loan interest, understand tenants' rights, gain access to health care and understand basic medical vocabulary, know how to get the facts he or she needs through research skills, read a magazine or newspaper and see the bias? It seems safe to say that if a person doesn't have the power to inform himself or herself with whatever is needed in a particular situation, he or she is illiterate.[7] In fact, the popular term *functional illiterate* refers to a person who is technically literate (can read at, let's say, a fourth-grade level or has completed the eighth grade) but is unable to read well enough to function successfully in society.[8]

So the next question is, what is "well enough to function successfully in society"?

The literacy demands of society have increased in recent years, and adults can't get by with rudimentary reading skills anymore. One hundred years ago being literate meant being able to write one's name; by those standards, nearly all adults are literate. Fifty years ago it meant being able to meet or exceed the performance of fourth-grade students; by those standards 95 percent of all native Americans are literate. Twenty-five years ago the standard of literacy was completion of the eighth grade; by that standard, 80 percent are literate.

But now—today—one in three American adults probably can't read and understand the average magazine article, which makes him or her illiterate. Not the old-fashioned illiterate who had to make an X instead of signing his name, but the "modern

[7] *Ibid.*
[8] Lisa Lin, "Illiteracy In America." *Seventeen*, Vol. 47, April 1988, p.99.

illiterate" who needs better reading skills than ever to function in today's world. Seventy percent of the reading material required in a cross section of jobs in the United States today is of between ninth- and twelfth-grade difficulty.[9] By the 1990s, warns Dorothy Shields, education director of the AFL-CIO, "anyone who doesn't have at least a twelfth-grade reading, writing, and calculating level will be completely lost."[10]

The chart below shows exactly how that translates into everyday life. How well do we need to read to "function in today's society"?[11]

| To Read and Understand | Reading Skill Level |
|---|---|
| Driver's license manual | 6th grade |
| Instructions on a frozen TV dinner | 8th grade |
| Directions on an aspirin bottle | 8th grade |
| Guide to social security benefits | 9th grade |
| An insurance policy | 12th grade |
| A typical newspaper article | 12th grade |
| An apartment lease | college |
| *To Hold a Job:* | |
| As a cook | 7th grade |
| As a mechanic | 8th grade |
| As a supply clerk | 10th grade |

How many "illiterates" are there?

[9] Marie Costa, *Adult Literacy/Illiteracy in the United States.* Santa Barbara: ABS-Clio, Inc., 1988, p.xviii.
[10] Quoted by Jonathan Kozol, *Illiterate America.* New York: Doubleday, 1985, p.58.
[11] Claire Safran, "Illiteracy: Read All About It." *Woman's Day*, October 1, 1986, p.87.

Because determining whether a person is illiterate depends so much on that person and his or her individual situation, it's impossible to know exactly how many "illiterates" there are. Several different estimates have been made, and all of them are appallingly high—high enough to urge some experts to call illiteracy "one of this nation's most serious diseases."[12] Here are some facts that may give you a general idea:

- According to the 1970 census, 1–1/2 million American adults can't read or write at all.[13]
- Twenty million adult Americans have such difficulty with reading that they can't satisfactorily answer all the questions on such simple forms as driver's license applications.[14]
- In one study, 14 percent of the cross section of adults surveyed couldn't write a check that would clear the bank; 13 percent couldn't address an envelope that could get to its destination; 28 percent couldn't figure out change for a $20 bill.[15]
- Fifty percent of today's young adult population can read and write but can't process complex information: locate correct information on complex displays of print, hold information in their memory while finding additional information, transform fragments of information

[12] Carl B. Smith and Leo C. Fay, *Getting People to Read*. New York: Delacorte Press, 1973, p.1.
[13] *Ibid.*
[14] *Ibid.*
[15] Kozol, *Prisoners of Silence*, p.1.

into new knowledge, write and communicate all of the above.[16]

• Twenty to 30 million of the 100 million adults (age 16 or over) in the American workforce have serious problems with basic skills—they can't read, write, calculate, solve problems, or communicate well enough to function effectively on the job or in their everyday lives; they can read but not well enough to use a reference book or understand a newspaper; they can write but not well enough to compose a business letter or fill out 10 percent of the questions on an application; they can compute but not well enough to balance a checkbook or prepare an invoice.[17]

• If eight years of schooling is the standard for functional literacy, 19 million Americans don't meet it; if the standard is twelve years, the figure becomes 70 million.[18]

• Five million job seekers are functionally illiterate.[19]

• The Center for Public Resources found that three quarters of the 184 corporations responding to a 1981 survey said that employee errors in reading, writing, and math had forced their companies to establish basic skills programs.[20] The Bell System alone estimated

[16] Kirsch and Jungeblut, p.12.
[17] Forrest P. Chisman, *Jump Start*. Southport Institute for Policy Analysis, January 1989, p.1.
[18] Smith and Fay, p.2.
[19] *Ibid.*
[20] NACAE, p.11.

in 1970 that its companies spent $25 million
on basic education for their employees.[21] The
nationwide price tag for such efforts exceeds
$10 billion.[22]

- In 1978 it was estimated that 30 percent of
Navy recruits were a danger to themselves
and to costly naval equipment because they
lacked basic educational skills.[23]
- In large metropolitan areas such as New York
and Chicago, one out of every four adults you
pass on the street is a nonreader.[24] On the
national level 1 percent are nonreaders and
6 percent read at the fourth-grade level or
below.[25]

## WHO ARE THESE PEOPLE?

Contrary to popular belief, these millions of struggling folks are not all immigrants and fourth-grade
dropouts on welfare. Some, of course, are.

- Forty-four percent of the adult black population and 56 percent of the Hispanic are functional or marginal illiterates.[26]
- One half of the heads of households below the
poverty line can't read an eighth-grade book.[27]

[21] Smith and Fay, p.2.

[22] NACAE, p.11.

[23] Kozol, *Prisoners of Silence*, p.4.

[24] Kozol, *Illiterate America*, p.1.

[25] Larry Mikulecky, "The Status of Literacy in Our Society," in
*Teaching Reading to Older Students*, Donald Bear, ed. Reno:
University of Nevada, 1989, p.2.

[26] Dr. Norvell Northcutt, quoted by Kozol, *Illiterate America*, p.2.

[27] *Ibid.*

- Of eight million unemployed adults, four to six million lack the skills to be retrained for hi-tech jobs.[28]
- More than half the adults on welfare are functionally illiterate.[29]
- Eighty-five percent of the juveniles who come before the courts are functionally illiterate.[30]
- Twenty-five percent of the adults in our prisons are functional illiterates.[31]

But we can't stereotype poor readers. They cover a broad spectrum of society. According to a 1986 national estimate, 51 percent of functional illiterates lived in small towns and suburbs, 41 percent in cities, and 8 percent in rural areas. Forty-one percent are English-speaking whites, 22 percent are English-speaking blacks, and 37 percent don't speak English at all (with 22 percent speaking only Spanish). Forty percent are between the ages of 20 and 39, 28 percent are between 40 and 59, and 32 percent are 60 or older.[32] No area of the country seems immune to illiteracy, either. In Prince George's County, Maryland, there are 30,000 adults who can't read above a fourth-grade level. Forty percent of the adult population of Boston is illiterate. In San Antonio, Texas, 152,000 adults are considered illiterate. In Utah, 200,000 adults lack the basic skills needed for employment.

---

[28] *Ibid.*
[29] Safran, p.86.
[30] *Ibid.*
[31] *Ibid.*
[32] Lin, p.99.

## WHY ARE SO MANY ADULTS ILLITERATE?

How can it be that in a civilized, advanced nation like ours, where education is free—mandatory, in fact—such a large proportion of the population can't read well enough to function in society? If there were just one answer for that, the problem could probably be solved in a matter of a few years. However, illiteracy has a number of sources, different for every person who suffers from it, which make the whole issue pretty complicated. It's a good idea, though, to sort through the major ones, just in case you and your parent are able to spot the culprit. Knowing why—determining whether he or she fell through the cracks or never had a floor to stand on in the first place[33]—can eliminate much of the feeling that, "It's all my fault and there's nothing I can do about it. I'm just stupid."

### LEARNING DISABILITIES

Undetected hearing or sight problems are often the cause of failure to learn to read in school. Actual learning disabilities, in which the brain has difficulty with certain aspects of processing stimuli or information, can be at the root of it, too. Today, if those problems are identified, special reading teachers can work with students to help them overcome the obstacles and get on with reading. But those techniques have not always been available to teachers, and in many schools special help is still not accessible to every child. It's no wonder, then, that if your

[33] Kozol, *Illiterate America*, p.64.

mom or dad suffered from some learning bugaboo, he or she may simply have been ignored, neglected, or diagnosed as "lazy" when a real physiological problem was at fault. One severe learning problem that has received a great deal of publicity in recent years is *dyslexia*. This disorder (technically called *developmental dyslexia* or *specific language disability*) prevents its victim from learning to real, spell, or write by ordinary teaching processes. The person with dyslexia sees letters on a page in a jumbled form. For example, when he sees the word "London," he may see "Ldonno," "Dnonol," or "Nodlno"—and perhaps even a different combination every time. Dyslexia is a physical condition, not a psychological problem or an excuse for laziness. It is caused by abnormalities in the cell structure of the brain in the areas that control language. There are actual differences in the anatomy of the brain of a dyslexic person from that of a nondyslexic. Although one in eight adults in the United States has dyslexia (that's 12 percent of the population)[34] and 23 million people have some degree of developmental dyslexia,[35] it has been recognized as a problem only for forty or fifty years, and not much more is known about it now than then. Those who have it are in good company—right along with people like Edison, Einstein, General Patton, and Woodrow Wilson—but they are often frightened, frustrated, and confused. Without the proper help, without the means to

[34] Susan Hampshire, *Susan's Story*. New York: St. Martin's Press, 1982, p.1.
[35] Louise Clarke, *Can't Read, Can't Write, Can't Talk Too Good Either*. New York: Walker and Company, 1973, p.34.

prove that they are as intelligent as everyone else, it can drastically change, even destroy, a life.

## PROBLEMS WITH OUR EDUCATIONAL SYSTEM WHEN YOUR PARENTS MAY HAVE BEEN IN SCHOOL

Around 1963, when more than likely your parents were populating the playground (and you were as yet undreamed of!), a decline in achievement, as measured by SAT, ACT, GRE, and elementary achievement test scores, began in the United States. Careful study of that decline has revealed that its cause was probably a thing called *progressive education*.

Progressive education, which started in the 1960s, called for:

- More emphasis on nonacademic education (courses like Family Relations instead of History).
- Expanded curriculum choices (not just English but Detective Stories and Monster Literature).
- Open classrooms and less grouping by ability.
- Relaxation of behavioral standards.
- Minimal homework.
- Promoting students who weren't ready for the next grade academically for fear of damaging them socially by keeping them back.
- Inflating grades and challenging students

less for fear of allowing them to fail and thus hurting their self-esteem.
• Weakening graduation requirements.

The result? By the 1970s remedial English courses became necessary for half the entering freshmen of some colleges.[36] A lack of discipline was exhibited in most schools. There was little evidence of the promotion of any positive values or attitudes. The system had failed so many who could have achieved so much more because it ignored (or was unaware of) the fact that before students can practice effective thinking—which is what progressive education was trying to promote—they need a command of essential tools, a store of reliable information. As one educator puts it, they were "trying to build a house from the roof downwards."[37]

Another problem with the educational system was the way reading was taught about the time your folks were learning to read. There was very little *phonics*, which is the technique of attacking new words, breaking them down, and sounding them out; instead a method called *look-say* was used. Proponents of the look-say method were trying to get kids to build a memory bank of words they could look at and recognize so that meaning could be stressed. The problem was that they were never taught how to break the code, and the teachers being trained in colleges at that time weren't being taught how to teach those word-attack skills. They could read words they were familiar with, but they

[36] NACAE, p.12.
[37] Bestor, quoted by NACAE, p.21.

never learned to decode words they hadn't seen before. Do you know how long it would take to be introduced to every word in the English language? That was on the elementary level. When they got to high school, your folks were probably faced with a myriad of minicourses in the English department that changed every six or nine weeks and had titles like, "Writing for Fun" and "Hip Poetry." None of those gave teachers a chance to interrelate reading, writing, and speaking, much less provide them with an opportunity to get to know their students and find out their special needs. They had to concentrate instead on being relevant, on turning students on, on avoiding discipline problems.

In short, education lost its authority, and as a result people like your mom and dad lost their chance at building the necessary skill bank to draw from in their lives. Many modern educators see it as a crime on the part of the school system. An editorial in *The Wall Street Journal* put it this way:

> We don't think the people who "reformed" American education over the past twenty years should be allowed to so easily forget that well after the problem [of progressive education] was recognized, tens of thousands of kids went over the falls and are now floating around in the workplace... making childlike errors in simple spelling, pronunciation, the reading of instructions, and arithmetic. As a result, they're consigned to seeking moronic jobs and enduring personal humiliation.[38]

---

[38] Quoted by NACAE from "Who Ruined the Schools." *Wall Street Journal*, May 12, 1983, p.42.

## PROBLEMS IN SOCIETY WHEN YOUR PARENTS MAY HAVE BEEN IN SCHOOL

Society was in pretty much of a mess around the time your folks may have been struggling to be able to read and write, and many experts feel that that had a definite effect on children's learning—or not learning.

For openers, the sixties and seventies saw the beginning of a great shift away from family. The divorce rate shot up, and more single parents were raising kids. More mothers had to work and could thus spend less time with their children, helping with homework, reading to them, and unconsciously building up a base of knowledge and experience necessary for learning. Many such parents were more concerned with their own problems than those of their kids and in fact relied on their children to be their buddies. That syndrome led to shortened childhoods, a real problem for learning. There is an important link between play and cognitive growth, language acquisition, problem-solving, and socialization. If kids' time for play was cut short—well, the implications for learning are obvious.

Then, of course, there was the major national rebellion against The Establishment, which was merely "the way our parents did things." The resulting loss of authority and increase in permissiveness contributed to illiteracy, many educators believe. Student protest and unrest, which led to more student control over schools and academic standards, caused those same students to suffer. Remedial courses had to be increased, and that in turn encouraged lowering of academic standards in high schools.

It was also a time of racial unrest, and although equal rights was a noble goal it tended to become distorted when it came to education. Schools began to provide rewards to minority students simply because they were minorities rather than because they had put forth effort and achieved. Thus, many minority children were promoted and even graduated because they were black, Indian, or Chinese, not because they could read, write, or add a simple column of figures.

Even the increased viewing of television that took place during the sixties had an effect on student (your parents') learning. While they were spending 8.5 percent of their time in school, most kids were spending 9 to 10 percent of their time in front of the television set. During the twenty years from 1960 to 1980 TV moved from eighth place to third place (out of ten) in order of influence on youths age thirteen to nineteen. This, experts say, reduced their attention span, stunted their academic development, and made them less patient with school and less adept at translating printed symbols into thoughts.[39] Television reduces the appeal of the printed word and creates the expectation that learning should always be easy and entertaining. It's tough to learn to read when you have those kinds of standards!

Finally, drug and alcohol use and abuse had its heyday at about that time and did a number on the heads of large numbers of learners. By 1974 drugs had moved from ninth place to fourth place in the

[39] NACAE, p.32.

Gallup Poll's listing of major problems confronting school systems. Between 33 and 82 percent of college students in 1970 were involved with drugs.[40] No one has to tell you what that does to the learning process.

## PERSONAL FACTORS

As we've said before, every adult with a reading problem is different and got where he or she is for a different reason. There are so many personal factors that could have influenced a nonreader in the early years that it's impossible to name them all, but a list of some very common clues might help in your understanding of your own parent:

- Growing up in a home where English wasn't the native language.
- Growing up in a home where there were no or few newspapers, magazines, books, encyclopedias, dictionaries.
- Parents who were themselves illiterate and thus couldn't help.
- Parents who were distraught, extremely busy, neglectful, or abusive and thus *wouldn't* help.
- Poor education—needed special help that wasn't there; had a vision or hearing problem that went undetected by the school; got off to a bad start, perhaps with an incompetent teacher; went to an overcrowded school and got shoved, forgotten, into a corner early on; had unpleasant experiences in school, such as

[40] *Ibid.*

having to read aloud and being laughed at in
the process.

- Interrupted education—missed a lot of school
because of illness or transience; changed
schools frequently and was never quite where
the other students were.
- Knowing he or she was going to pursue an
occupation for which an education wasn't vital
and so never taking learning seriously.
- Poor economic situation at home, which had
an effect on interests and motivations and
aspirations—and thus on progress in learning.

If you look closely at that list, it might be a little
scary for you. This is a description of what *their*
homes were like growing up. Do they sound like
the home *you* are growing up in, too? Is illiteracy
"hereditary"?

Failure to see literacy as an important factor in
happiness and satisfaction and success in life *can*
be something that's passed down through genera-
tions—but it doesn't *have* to be. The very fact that
you're reading this book means you're aware of the
dangers, and that's half the battle. Now for the other
half. What do you do about it?

The following chapter deals with how you can
help your mom or dad find the professional help he
or she needs and how you can help at home. The
only way to stop a vicious circle is to put your foot
right in there and throw it out of whack. Have you
got those toes ready?

# CHAPTER ◇ 5

# Help!

J ack is a fifty-five-year-old plumber who until two years ago didn't know the alphabet. The child of a chronically ill mother and an alcoholic father, Jack dropped out of school at age twelve but was always able to hide his inability to read, even from his wife and children. When he finally lost a job after being unable to take a test on safety procedures, he approached his wife with his problem, and she urged him to get help. A TV commercial for a local reading program steered them in the right direction, and after two years Jack is reading on a second-grade level. He still hides his illiteracy from his new employer, sneaking out to his truck during lunch and coffee breaks to work on reading cards, but with others he's open about his goals. He wants to be able to read to his granddaughter, select from a menu rather than ordering the specials, send his wife a card instead of a flower. The first letter he writes when he's able to is going to be to his family— to tell them how much he loves them.

\* \* \*

Paul is not the stereotypical "illiterate." He's white, middle class, and thirty-something, is a high school graduate, and wears Levis and Reeboks. But when he started working with a reading tutor he read at a third-grade level, and he had difficulty raising that level at first because years of shame and repeated failures had made him afraid he simply couldn't learn. After a year with his college-age tutor, Paul has had a series of firsts: getting a library card, reading a letter from his father, filling out a job application—reading his son's report card.

When June graduated from high school she couldn't read her diploma. Nor could she read street signs, want ads, or menus with "long and fancy words"—like cheeseburger. She grew up one of six children in a troubled, disorganized family and was unable to concentrate at school because of home problems. No one really noticed, and she spent most of elementary school sitting and coloring. When she got to high school she simply told her teachers, "Don't call on me to read because I can't." When she married, her husband read restaurant menus to her, helped her with the shopping, and filled out her application for a minimum-wage factory job. She always felt that there was something wrong with her that had kept her from learning to read, and she had resigned herself to living with it—until she had kids. Then it became unbearable. She couldn't read to them, couldn't communicate with their teachers, couldn't get them anywhere on time because she couldn't figure out instructions and addresses. Her oldest, Kelly, was twelve when June could stand it no longer. She was staring helplessly at the phone book when Kelly came along and helped her look up the number of the library. Then Kelly dialed it for her, went with her to sign up for a tutor, and helped her with her homework. When June was able to read the guidelines Kelly brought home for cheerleader tryouts, she and Kelly went out and celebrated. And when they did, June read the menu for herself.

There isn't anyone who can't be helped with a literacy problem—no matter how old they are or what path they've walked in their lives or what caused them to fail to learn to read in the first place. Help is there. The biggest problem is usually finding the courage to reach out and get that help. But as you can see from these people's stories, the biggest motivator is usually the family.

As a teenage son or daughter, you can probably do more than almost anybody to assist your parent in getting the help he or she needs with a reading problem. You may just need a few suggestions and some encouragement—and that's what this chapter is all about.

## HOW TO APPROACH A PARENT ABOUT GETTING HELP

The first step in dealing with a literacy problem is also the hardest: admitting that there *is* a problem. Teachers in adult reading programs say students who come in even for the first interview will smoke three cigarettes before they can get out why it is they've come. Many say they dialed the number eighteen times in two weeks before finally holding on long enough for someone to answer. It's a milestone just to make the call.

We're talking about a deeply rooted problem here. Many adults in this situation are completely convinced that they can't learn to read because there was no literacy in *their* home growing up. They may be absolutely certain that they're not smart enough to make it. They may have struggled so long through grade school that they have a total mental block. All of that can be knocked down, but it takes a lot of time and a lot of work.

And it isn't appealing work, either. It's very likely that when your parent failed in school he or she was always placed in the "Dinky Birds" reading group (as opposed to the "Cardinals" or the "Bluejays"). She probably had to repeat the same books over and over and do stupid, inane drills until she learned to hate *More Fun with Dick and Jane*, she learned to hate teachers, she learned to hate the very sight of words.

What you're faced with if you want to help your parents, then, is helping them own up to the problem, gather the courage to seek help, and see that this time it's going to be different. That's a tall order, but some guidelines might be helpful to you.

***Realize how hard this is for them.*** If you can empathize, your mom or dad will realize that it is possible to be understood, that if his or her kid can see the problem and yet still respect him, maybe this won't be so bad. But empathy takes a real understanding of the problem. Dr. Donald Bear, a professor at the University of Nevada–Reno who directs clinics and tutorial programs at the university, suggested thinking of facing a reading problem as a "toe-pinching phenomenon." When a person is confronted with something threatening (in this case, having to read or admit that he can't read) he tends to react as if someone is stepping on his toe. He becomes regressive, anxious, and tense and finally just pulls away. If you can relate to how that feels, if you can understand that this is a whole lot tougher than making a doctor's appointment, you'll be able to say, "Dad, I know this is going to be hard, but I think I know where your head is on this." And then you'll be able to help.

***Try to pinpoint where your mom or dad is coming from.*** There are several different types of adults with reading problems. Some recognize the value of literacy and are motivated to acquire it; they have confidence that they can make a difference in their own lives. They just need some direction. Others are interested in learning but don't see literacy as directly relevant to what they want to learn. They just need the right program. Still others, because of fear, past failure, or hopelessness, seem to have no desire to learn or just think they can't. These may include non-English speakers who, literate in their own language or not, have been convinced by the social system that they are socially and economically expendable[1]—so what's the point?

If you can figure out where your mom or dad falls in this scheme of things, you'll know better what approach to take in helping him or her. If Dad is motivated, it could be a piece of cake. If Mom wants to learn but doesn't see how it's going to get her

[1] Jonathan Kozol, *Prisoners of Silence*. New York: Continuum Publishing Corporation, 1980, p.5.

anywhere, you can help her see the relevance and get her into a program that concentrates on practical skills. If your parent is completely down and out or doesn't speak English at all, you'll know the going will be tougher and you'll take a different approach—one laced with plenty of encouragement and support.

*Make respect the name of the game.*   Your mother or father has experienced enough humiliation in having a reading problem without a teenage son or daughter saying, "Good grief, get on the stick and do something about this! What's your problem?" Your approach in saying, "There's help out there. Let's get some for you," has to have the ring of respect. It also has to say, "I look up to you. I'm proud of you. I love you, and I want what's best for you." If you can convince your folks that you hold them in even higher esteem because they're trying to better themselves, you've got it made.

*Be ready with sound reasoning.*   All the facts you've been given in this book will aid you in convincing your parent that improving literacy is vital. However, the offspring of poor and nonreaders who have aided their parents in getting back to school say the following have been the most helpful to them.

*"Illiteracy has nothing to do with intelligence."*   You aren't stupid, Dad. You're one of the smartest guys I know. But you could use your intelligence so much more if you could read better.

*"You're good at so many other things."*   Just because you can't read that well, Mom, doesn't mean

you're no good. Check out that sewing. You're always helping somebody. Geez, you're a great organizer. You're so bright and talented. You could do so much more, be so much happier if you had better reading skills.

*"You can get rid of all this stuff that's standing in your way."* It's a false claim that anyone who becomes literate is automatically better off, immediately able to find employment, instantly a better citizen,[2] but it is almost impossible in our society to lead a life of self-satisfaction and productivity if you can't read.[3] Even if you can read some—you're what is called mid-level literate—not being able to learn fast from written materials in training programs or in on-the-job learning sessions can really strain your capabilities.[4]

*"You could feel so much better about yourself."* Many people are referred to reading programs by psychologists as a way to do something about their low self-esteem. I hate to see you backing off in conversation because you're afraid your "ignorance" might show, when you have so much to offer other people.

*"It works!"* Look at Susan Hampshire. She is a complete dyslexic, but she's had a brilliant acting

[2] National Advisory Council on Adult Education, *Illiteracy in America.* Washington D.C.: U.S. Government Printing Office, p.11.
[3] Donald Bear, ed. *Teaching Reading to Older Students.* Reno: University of Nevada, 1989, p.1.
[4] Irwin S. Kirsch and Ann Jungeblut, *Literacy Profiles of America's Young Adults.* Princeton: Educational Testing Service, 1986, p.2.

career in Britain in spite of her horrendous problems with reading—because she got help. She has one of the worst of all possible problems to contend with and made it. For you it should be Simple City! Yeah, if a person is totally illiterate, it takes several hundred hours of instruction to be able to meet daily functional literacy demands. But for somebody who reads at, say, a fourth-grade level already, it only takes fifty to 150 hours.[5] What's that if it can change your life?

*"Just because you aren't literate in English doesn't mean that who you were in your own country is lost."* You are still that person. You don't have to be like the Saudi Arabian engineer who because he can't read English works as a busboy in the United States. There is special help for non-English speakers who are well educated in their own language and culture. Let's break through all this alienation and shyness and insecurity that have built up and make it here, too. Let's buoy that self-esteem back up again.

*"This isn't just going to help you—it's going to help me."* That's the kind of parent you are—you want to do what's right for your kids. If we have a more highly literate home, it can only make my future brighter, right along with yours. (This is your ace. Reading instructors say that more adults enroll in classes because of their kids than for any other reason.)

---

[5] Bear.

\*     \*     \*

Carla, whose father is basically illiterate in English and in his native Spanish, was the one responsible for getting him into an ESL class where he is learning to speak and read English. "It was hard to say, 'Dad, you need to go to school!' But as a teenager you're adult enough to talk to your folks. And it's worth it. I knew that the first time Dad looked up at the menu in Burger King and ordered his own lunch. It's a small thing—but for him, for us, it was pretty big."

## HOW TO FIND A GOOD PROGRAM

There are many different types of adult reading programs, which is fortunate since there are so many different types of poor and nonreaders! Before we get into specifics, though, it's a good idea to list the characteristics that all good, effective programs have in common:

- Someone who will just talk to the student first rather than diving immediately into a pretest or workbook. This is vital for finding out what personal factors have been involved in the person's inability to learn to read thus far and for making him or her feel comfortable rather than embarrassed or ashamed. Every person has to feel relaxed and unthreatened before any learning can take place.
- Meaningful instruction—something that relates to him or her as an individual. A bunch of drills isn't going to cut it. Dad needs to deal with the words that relate to his job. Mom needs to hone in on practical things—recipes,

labels, shopping lists, things that connect to her job. Yes, they have to do exercises in workbooks and learn phonics—but they shouldn't do only that for six months with never a trace of how this is all going to improve their lives. If the program doesn't come close to the skills they personally need to function effectively, they won't retain what they're learning or stay with the program.

- Teachers who are willing to be friends as well as instructors and who will treat your parents with respect and dignity. Remember that your mom or dad has probably come to view teachers somewhat like bill collectors. The same kinds of fears and resentments have probably built up over the years, and they aren't going to be easy to erase unless the new teacher is warm, caring, and admiring of your mom or dad's courage and determination. One indicator of lack of respect is a tendency to correct how the student *speaks*; if you hear that, get out of there.
- Well-trained volunteers, if volunteers are used. Not everyone who is himself able to read is qualified to teach someone else to read. Ask how many hours of instruction volunteers have had and how much experience. You do have the right, you know!
- No unrealistic promises. There is no quick fix for a reading problem. It's always a long-term commitment, a long haul. If someone guarantees that in thirty days your dad will be reading on the college level, grab Dad and run!
- A sliding scale or no cost at all. Why pay a lot of money when charging big bucks doesn't

indicate a good program? The very best that are out there right now require little or no payment. Go for those.

- For an adult who reads very little already, a one-on-one teaching situation. This can expand to six or seven in a class later on, but for openers the nonreader needs privacy and undivided attention.
- For an adult who doesn't speak English, a teacher of the same ethnic background.
- For an adult who has been diagnosed as having a learning disability such as dyslexia, a teacher or program versed in that particular problem. Dyslexics, for example, must be taught using color and shape and have to go back to primers and phonics. The techniques are very specialized and require certain training. Those who have worked with folks with severe learning problems know the emotional defeat, humiliation, and frustration that has been endured, too, and can treat that as well.
- Hours and location that are convenient. The best program in the world is no good if the student can't get there!

Once you know what kind of program you're looking for, where do you start? Try this list of suggestions:

- Watch for TV ads that give hotline numbers. These aren't shams—they're community services.
- Ask the reading specialist at your own school.
- Call the local community college. Be sure to tell them exactly how bad the problem is, so that they can steer you to the right program.

- Look up Adult Basic Education in the phone book. It's sometimes listed under a college.
- Contact the alternative high school in your area if there is one. They often have adult programs.
- Look up and call any of the volunteer literacy organizations listed in the Appendix.
- Call your library. If they don't have a program, they can probably tell you where to find one.

The options are almost endless once you get in there and start looking. Don't give up until you find the help you need. If the first program Dad tries is a bummer, help him find another one. Pat tried two before she found the private tutor who has brought her up six grade levels in eighteen months. Bill went to three different classes before Reading Plus at his local library brought him up five in two years. Unfortunately, adult literacy programs attract less than 7 percent of those who need help and have a dropout rate of 50 to 70 percent.[6] Most of those who drop out never look for another program. Don't let your folks become one of those statistics.

## HOW YOU CAN HELP AT HOME

We're not talking here about your becoming your mom's or dad's private tutor. The average teen isn't qualified to attack that kind of problem, and even if he were, chances are it just wouldn't work with Mom and Dad. Carla is a paid aide in the same

[6] Rosemarie J. Park, "Three Approaches to Improving Literacy Levels," in *Teaching Reading To Older Students*, Donald Bear, ed. Reno: University of Nevada, 1989, p.106.

program her parents are enrolled in, but at home when she attempts to carry on with the lessons she hears, "You aren't doing it right! You didn't give me a chance!" It's a lot like the stories you hear of a husband trying to teach his wife to drive—it rarely happens without somebody slamming a door and stomping off!

The kind of help we're referring to here is more in the area of support of what's already going on at school, and that's as vital to your parents' success as their support of your schoolwork is to your success. The following suggestions come from the experts: teachers, scholars of adult reading, and the real pros—parents and kids who've been there.

***Be consistently understanding.*** According to Dr. Donald Bear, 99 percent of the time a person's reading problem is just a mental block. It takes more than a good program to knock that down. It takes love and understanding, and who can give your parent more of that than you can? "I know it's tough." "I bet you do get frustrated sometimes." "You must feel like it's never going to get any better. I can understand that." They want to hear that as much as you want to hear, "I know it's rough being a teenager, but it isn't going to last forever!"

***Never, never embarrass them.*** If you of all people add to the shame they already feel, the whole thing is a bust. Don't talk about the fact that they're back in school with people outside the family unless your parent gives the okay. Don't put them on the reading spot in public. Don't even tease them about it when it's just the two of you unless you know that sets well with them. This is delicate territory. Tread carefully.

*Praise every new accomplishment.* Your mom or dad will need to know you're proud. People who enter adult reading programs are often not typical learners (or else they might have learned to read in grade school). They don't learn easily in abstracting meaning from printed symbols, so they're faced with a very difficult task. You know what that's like. Didn't you feel pretty insecure and negative about yourself when you struggled with algebra for the first time? Tried to learn to dance or hit a baseball? First asked a girl out, for Pete's sake? Put yourself in that place and then multiply it times one hundred and then give your mom and dad enough encouragement to cover that.

*Help out with practical stuff.* Many instructors say there's a high dropout rate in adult reading classes because of child-care problems. Can you help out there? Can you curtail your own social life a little and take care of the younger kids on the nights Mom goes to class? Can you get the little rug rats out of the house when she's trying to do her homework? Even if there aren't toddlers and tykes around, there are other day-to-day chores that can conflict with a parent's schooling that you can take over or help with. Can you cook dinner on class nights? Do some laundry? Drive your mother to class? Take a cut in allowance so she can have that extra bus fare to get to class? Think about how you can lighten the load for a working parent who is holding down a job, trying to run a household, and raising kids, and is now adding school to that already impossible load.

*Make your home a richly literate place.* Learning to read, says Donald Bear, mimics learning to talk.

If you're in a richly literate environment you'll learn to read (unless there is something organically wrong or you've experienced an "educational insult"). So create that environment for your folks. Buy magazines and leave them on the coffee table. Pick up free pamphlets on subjects your parent is into and make them available. Check appropriate books (things that aren't too hard for them) out of your school library when you're there doing homework or watching the boys. Two good predictors of reading success in children are whether they're read to and whether there are books around for them to look at. If those two things are present, we learn to read in spite of how we're taught. The same can be true for your parents.

If you think your parents will respond to your being more direct in your help, try some of these ideas. Have a story hour and read to your parents when they're first starting out, and later have them read to you. Keep your eyes open for appropriate reading material for that. Leave notes for your folks—on their level, of course. When they want to write a letter, have them dictate to you and write exactly what they say; then read it back and let them help you edit. Help them keep an address book. Write out simple form letters for them to use as models when they want to write a complaint about a bill, order something from a catalog, or say thank you to somebody. Make up prototypes of frequently used forms for them to use when they want to apply for a job, make an insurance claim, place an order. Play word games like "Boggle" and "Scrabble."

One of the most important things you can do is be a model for your parents. Read yourself—as much as you can—where they can see you. When their reading skills start to improve, share what you're reading with them. Nothing makes people feel prouder of what they're learning than being able to discuss it on an intelligent level—even if it's an article in *Reader's Digest*.

This may all seem a little absurd to you. After all, as an adolescent you're supposed to be finding your independence and breaking away from the old bonds a little as you discover who you are and turn into an adult—and here we are suggesting that you get even more involved in your parents' life! Nobody's saying abandon your growing up for the time being while your mom or dad learns to read. What we are saying is that adolescence is also a time of maturing, and nothing helps you mature more than to become aware of someone else's need and to attend to it with love. When a parent is learning to read or trying to improve his or her present reading skills, it becomes a family project. Adults in tutoring programs who *have* kids in school tend to stay longer in the programs than others just because they *have* kids. If those kids are also actively involved in the process, the chances that the learning will continue are even greater. If you are *involved*—that's real maturity on your part. In the midst of going to school yourself, playing on the basketball team, hanging out with your friends, there's still time to say, "Go for it, Dad." "Hey, Mom, did you read that piece in *People* about Tom Cruise?" "You guys—I'm impressed with what you're doing."

The results are worth it. Wally's mother and father are divorced, and his father lives a thousand miles away. Until his father took up with a reading tutor, Wally got a card a year that was signed "Dad." Now his father writes him letters and calls him more often because he has things he's proud to talk about. Wally could never communicate with his father before; now he's gotten to the point where he can tease him about only being "in seventh grade" when Wally himself is a junior. He knows his father can hear the pride in his voice.

Carla did everything for her non-English-speaking parents until they applied for the amnesty program and were required to learn English. She found the class for them and went with them to help them sign up. At home she encourages them, asks them what they're learning, speaks English to them. Their classes have taught her to urge them to do more for themselves, and that has given her a chance to do more with her own life.

Pat has never hidden from her two young sons the fact that she is in school learning to read just as they are. She has also taught them not to look down on her for it or be ashamed of her or treat her with any less respect. Probably most important, she's taught them the importance of each little accomplishment in a person's life. If you complete *something*, they now know, you can be proud of that.

It has been found that one of the best ways to improve the reading performance of children is to improve the education level of their parents. By helping your parents get the schooling they need and by encouraging them at home, their skills improve, and in the long run so do yours. As a result, you're not only helping your parents, you're helping yourself, your brothers and sisters—and even your own future children.

# CHAPTER 6

# How to Cope

O nce they became involved in helping their parents to start improving their literacy skills, most of the young people we've talked with figured that their own troubles connected with their parents' reading problems were over. Most of them were wrong.

When Mark's father started working with a reading tutor, he became more and more eager to talk about what he was doing. Mark was embarrassed when he said stuff around his friends like, "You guys don't know how lucky you are to be getting the kind of education you're getting. Take advantage of it. Don't wait 'til you're an old man like me and have to get into 'See Spot run'!" Mark stopped bringing his friends around when his dad was home.

Pam didn't realize how low her mother's skills were until she saw some of her homework. It got harder to maintain respect, and she found herself looking down on her mother—and showing it. She heard more, "Don't get smart with me, young lady," than she ever had.

Billy just felt, when it was all out in the open, that

his family was somehow different, maybe abnormal, and definitely inferior. What, he wondered, did that make him?

Let's face it: Any problem that affects a member of your family affects you. Your next step is to take a good look at the difficulties a literacy problem in one of your parents creates for you and find out how to cope with those difficulties. Of course, no two people are exactly alike, so not all of the feelings and pitfalls we'll talk about here apply to everyone. It may even be that you've got a handle on the thing and none of this relates to your situation. We just offer you some suggestions we've received from professionals and families and hope you'll take those that strike a chord in you.

## OWN UP TO YOUR FEELINGS

Since a lot of what you feel when you find out that your mom or dad is a stranger to the written word is negative, it sometimes seems a whole lot easier— and *nicer* on your part—to stash it away someplace and pretend it doesn't exist. But all feelings, no matter how negative, are okay. You have a reason for having them, they belong to you, and they're nothing to be ashamed of. Now, how you deal with them is another matter, and we'll talk about that, too, but first let's take a look at the inner struggles that are common among the offspring of illiterate or nearly illiterate parents.

*Shame:* You love your dad but you are embarrassed when you see him staring at the estimate for having the car fixed and know he's only understanding about half of it. Adolescence notwithstanding, you'd like to be proud of your parents—not ashamed to have them meet your teachers!

***Superiority and lack of respect:*** No matter how good your mother is at other things, if she struggles just to decipher the directions on the back of the macaroni and cheese you may find yourself snatching the package out of her hand, sighing heavily, and saying in a martyred tone, "I'll do it." You may have trouble looking up to someone who doesn't even come close to your skill in reading and writing, and when you have trouble looking up, there's no where to look but down.

***Fear:*** All kinds of fears are attached to having a nonreading parent. Fear of winding up in the same dead-end kind of job and life-style, even if you yourself read well. Fear of somebody finding out and judging your parent, you, your whole family. Fear that your parent will somehow let you down when you need him because he doesn't have the required skills. When "failure" is involved, it gets scary.

***Feeling "different":*** You're a teenager. It's in your contract to want to fit in and not be a weirdo. A family where Dad works as a janitor because he can't read well enough to get a job doing what he really wants to do, or where Mom is bent on hiding the fact that she's never read a newspaper, written a letter, or communicated with anyone about anything on a higher level than what happened on the last episode of "Falcon Crest"—and claims that, dammit, she doesn't want to—that's enough to make you feel like a case of acne on the complexion of life. Why can't your family be like every other family,

with magazines lying around and fathers grunting
behind newspapers and mothers writing you notes
saying, "Went to class. Dinner's in the frig"? Feeling
different, abnormal, and inferior is a drag.

## DEAL WITH YOUR FEELINGS PRODUCTIVELY

All of those feelings are not only common, they're
understandable. Very few people in your position
can get through it all without some shame, embarrassment, fear, or disdain. However, just because
your feelings are perfectly natural doesn't mean
they're easy. Wanting to hide every time your parent darkens the door of your school or wondering
daily if you, too, are going to spend your life waiting
tables is not fun. Fortunately, you don't have to just
live with it. There are productive ways to handle
what's going on inside you.

*The shame.* Just because you feel shame doesn't
mean that realistically you have anything to be
ashamed of. Look at the facts again. Your parent's
inability to read well has nothing to do with her
intelligence, nor did it happen through any fault
of hers. It is basically nothing for your dad himself to be ashamed of, so why should it be for you?
No, thinking that way isn't going to instantly snuff
out your embarrassment, but if you repeat those
thoughts to yourself it can help you keep things in
perspective. It's also good to keep in mind that
other people are probably not as aware of the problem as you think they are. After all, how long did it
take you to find out—and you live with this person!

So if it's "what other people think" that's bothering you, relax.

*The superiority and disdain.* Concentrate on the things Mom or Dad does well. Everybody has something they excel in. Maybe your father can't read worth a flip, but what about his natural business savvy, his common sense, the fine craftsmanship of his carpentry? Besides, he's doing the toughest job going, which is raising you to be the kind of person who would bother to pick up this kind of book in the first place! When you get right down to it, your parents are your parents, no matter what their problems. If you can keep in focus that just getting you this far is grounds for respect, it'll be easier not to look down on them for what are currently their shortcomings. Take some action on that. Tell Mom she's great cook. Mention to Dad that as much as you hate to admit it he does give you good advice. It'll make the going easier for you.

*The fear.* The first step in dealing with fear is to stand back, look at the situation, and see if there's really anything to be afraid of. Try asking yourself, "What's the worst that can happen?" If somebody finds out that your father is a functional illiterate, what's the worst that can happen? Will you immediately become a social outcast? Be dropped from the National Honor Society? Find yourself suddenly minus a prom date? When Carla finally told a few of her closest friends that neither of her parents could read in English or Spanish, she found that they were completely supportive and she began to feel more comfortable with letting other people know if a situation arose where it seemed appropriate. Only once during her entire high school career did anyone say, "Well, why don't they just learn?" Then she found herself defending her folks for all she was worth!

As for the fear of ending up with the same kinds of problems as your nonreading parents—inheriting a legacy, so to speak, you have already practically sealed a guarantee that that isn't going to happen. You read well enough to read this book *and* you have the motivation and resourcefulness to read the facts that will help you solve your problems. Those are qualities inherent in successful people.

Folks who have been there simply say, don't let fear get in your way. "You're unique," says Pat. "Don't let your parents' problems stop you. Don't wait until you're thirty to improve yourself. Don't pass it on to your kids. Get your education now!"

Marcos, who was three when his father died, grew up with a bilingual mother who always seemed to be in too much emotional turmoil to read to him or, as he got older, supervise his homework. He didn't realize until he was in high school that she *couldn't* read and had always used the excuse, "I'm too upset," or "I'm too tired," to cover it up. By then, Marcos wasn't in much better shape himself. He couldn't read very well, was convinced he never would be able to, and resigned himself to living in the same economic conditions his mother lived in. In his sophomore year a concerned teacher befriended Marcos, learned about his family situation, and got both Marcos and his mother into a reading program. At about the same time Marcos stumbled into a small nonspeaking role in a school play and got the stage bug. Armed with motivation and support and the encouragement of seeing his mother learn, Marcos began to leap over reading levels like an Olympian. Now a freshman in college, he acts in university theatrical productions, gaining roles through cold readings, and is determined to have a future on the stage. Whether he will or not is beside the point. He sees that there are options and possibilities for him—and for his mother.

***The Feeling of "inferiority."***　Turn off those television sitcoms and wake up to reality: There are no standards for the "normal" family, and if there were, no family but the one setting them would fit them because every family is different. What makes each one different is that each one has its own set of problems. Some deal with long-term illness, some unemployment, some divorce, some abuse, others drugs and alcohol, still others religious conflict—the list is endless. In your family the problem is literacy. That doesn't make you any less loving, any less important, any less worthy to breathe the air, for Pete's sake! Besides, yours is a problem that can be solved, not just coped with. If you and your family take this thing by the horns, that actually brings you a cut above the average.

## FIND A WAY TO EXPRESS YOUR FEELINGS

It doesn't matter what the problem is, if you can't get it out somehow it's going to fester within like a giant zit. You'll find yourself bickering with your parents, withdrawing from the family, or giving up entirely. Whatever healthy thing you can do to express or work through what's eating at you, do it. Write in a journal. Work out. Run. Get involved in sports or a chorus or a dance class. Just don't let uglies build up.

## FIND SOMEONE YOU CAN TALK TO

A lot of what you're feeling can be dealt with just by having a chance to run it by somebody. There are many people—even adults—who don't know they really think something until they've said it. If you can, find an adult you trust that you can chat with from time to time about how coming from a household with an illiterate parent is affecting you. It doesn't have to be somebody who necessarily has a lot of answers, but simply an older friend who is willing to listen and help you steer your thinking in the right direction. A guidance counselor, a teacher you especially like and respect, your boss at work, an aunt or uncle, that sixty-five-year-old neighbor who's retired and likes to jaw with you when you go out to get into your car. If that person's responses are pretty much in line with what we've said in this book, you've got yourself a good ear. Call it a support group of one if you like, but use it. All of us need a shoulder and a resounding "Go for it!" once in a while.

## COMMUNICATE WITH YOUR PARENTS

Most parents would hate more than anything for their kids to go through an emotional struggle alone. It's okay to talk to your folks about your wishes for them and consequently for all of you as a family. As we've said before, that doesn't mean going up to your dad and saying, "You can't read and it has really screwed me up. Good grief, do something about it!" It may mean saying, "It really hurts to see you letting all that talent go to waste just because you have a literacy problem that can be solved", or, "I know you're going to classes for reading but I'm having a hard time getting past, 'God! What if somebody finds out?' I'm proud of you, but it's hard." Whenever a family is faced with a problem, communication is vital to working it out. Shame cuts off communication.[1] Don't let that happen. Talk about it if you can.

## Think Positive

Don't you hate it when people toss out clichés like that? It's as bad as having a store clerk you never saw before telling you to "Have a nice day."

But in this case "Think positive" is more than a cliché. It's the only way to see beyond the hours of instruction your parent faces and the stuff you have to cope with while he does. Illiteracy is treatable, but it can mean a lifelong struggle over things like learning disabilities and deeply rooted mental blocks. Nobody who has a negative attitude, or who has a kid with a negative attitude about it, is going to make it. Every part of the effort has to be turned into something good. You have to face facts and yet also be something of a Pollyanna about them. You may be the only other person in the house who can talk your mom into going to class when she's just worked a nine-hour day, had a flat tire, and nursed a headache that was "this big" through the whole thing. You can only get her out of the house, book in hand, if you have a "You can do it" look in your eye

[1] Donald Bear, Ph.D., University of Nevada, Reno, January 1989.

and a "Go get 'em, Tiger" tone in your voice. Use young actor Carl Evans as your inspiration. Carl plays teen hunk Alan-Michael Spaulding on the daytime drama "Guiding Light." He has to read and memorize 175 or more pages of dialog a week and does so in spite of his dyslexia. So he's learned to compensate and feels that because of his learning disorder he's a better actor. Reading his scenes over and over again, as he is forced to do, helps him, he feels, flesh out his character. "I have an understanding that lets me take a scene places where it might not have gone," he says.[2] That's what we mean by a positive attitude.

If as a teenager you can cope with the by-products of illiteracy in your home, you'll enter adulthood way ahead of the maturity game. You'll already know how to attack a problem and get the best of it, how to express your feelings about touchy subjects with people you love and maintain your self-esteem— and help someone you love maintain theirs—in spite of a handicap other people may have looked down their noses at. You'll be able to handle just about anything—and in the bargain, you and your soon-to-be-a-reading-parent will be a whole lot closer.

[2] TV Guide, February 1989, p.26.

# CHAPTER 7

# Rebel Children

In a recent episode of CBS's sitcom "Kate and Allie," Kate discovered that the building's super, Lou, was a closet illiterate. The show centered around Lou's all-too-common dilemma and was followed by a taped message from First Lady Barbara Bush, urging Americans to combat illiteracy and giving a toll-free number to call for those seeking or offering help.

When you see efforts like that coming through prime-time TV, you realize that America is waking up to the problem of literacy and is trying to do something about it. But as we've seen, the problem is so large, so complex, and so personal that it's going to take every American's waking up to really begin to pull us out of the mire of poor reading and writing skills.

"Every American" includes you.

Give me a break, you may say. Sure, I can help my own mom or dad, but what can I do about it on a national level? I'm a kid!

No one expects you to call Barbara Bush and volunteer your services. However, you can take some responsibility, even now, even in a tiny way. If each of you—at age twelve or fourteen or eighteen—accepts that responsibility and goes with it, today's adults who are unaware of the literacy problem or who ignore it will have to take notice. When you take over society (sooner than you think!) you won't be guilty of that same ignorance.

If you need more motivation than that, perhaps Jonathan Kozol provides it. In his *Prisoners of Silence*, to which we've referred several times in this book, he insists that young people—like you—can be the ethical spearheads of society. He says adolescence isn't a moratorium on life during which you sit around waiting to grow up before you form or express any opinions. It's a portion of life. So, he goes on, you can be an effective actor on the stage of history now by actively participating in the literacy campaign.[1] It's in your contract as a teenager to have energy and idealism. Use it. As a generation, be the "rebel children"[2] of society and help break the cycle of illiteracy.

How?

Some guidelines might help.

## LEARN AS MUCH AS YOU CAN ABOUT ILLITERACY

The literacy problem is so complex and has so many facets and levels and causes that it's been impossible for us to cover it completely in this book. You really need to educate yourself more fully by reading

[1] Jonathan Kozol, *Prisoners of Silence*. New York: Continuum Publishing Corporation, 1980, pp.92–94.
[2] *Ibid.*, p.98.

everything on the subject that comes your way—
newspaper and magazine articles, brochures you
find in libraries and bookstores, and paying attention to what we're seeing in the broadcast media—
commercials and coverage on TV "magazine shows"
(like "60 Minutes") and treatment on series (like
"Kate and Allie"). After all, the first step in solving
any problem is to understand what you're fixing.

No time to delve that deeply into a subject? Kill
the proverbial two bluejays with one piece of the
rock. Next time you have to write a research paper
or do a speech for a class, select the literacy problem
as a topic. You'll be amazed at how really educating
yourself—as opposed to just going through the mo-
tions and doing a paper on the exports of Romania—
will make you feel!

## DEVELOP A GENERAL ATTITUDE ABOUT THE SUBJECT

Being a campaigner for literacy is not something you
slap on from the outside like a bumper sticker. It has
to come from within, so that it shows when people
make uneducated comments like, "Well, why didn't
they just learn to read when they were supposed
to?" or I don't need to be able to read and write that
good. I just want to work construction." Below
you'll find some statements that, if you find they
make sense, you might want to make part of your set
of beliefs about literacy.

***We have to be a literate nation in order to protect
our freedoms.***   Personal freedom took its first giant

steps when the general population began to learn to read. Without the printing press and the consequent spread of the Protestant Reformation, John Locke's essays, Thomas Paine's writings, and the Declaration of Independence (which, by the way, is written on an eleventh-grade level) for the people to read, the better part of us might still be serfs! You know— no choosing your career, your spouse, your pizza toppings, for Pete's sake! Without being able to read, we can't really keep an eye on how our government is being run and what laws are being passed right under our noses. Sure, we have the six o'clock news, but even the anchorman will tell you that "World News Tonight" can only scratch the surface. If we want to stay free, each of us has to be fully literate.

*Illiteracy is unacceptable.*   That doesn't mean that an illiterate person is unacceptable! It does mean that none of us should pass illiteracy off as a routine handicap—"Yeah, a lot of people are that way. They just can't learn to read."—or as something that's "okay." It isn't "okay" any more than diabetes or muscular dystrophy is okay. Sure, people can learn to live with it, but why should they have to if we can fight to eradicate it? Accepting without question anything that keeps any person from being the best he or she can be is dangerous to us all.

*Literacy is essential for a complete, satisfying life.*
Gone are the days when the "simple folk" could get along just fine making an X for a signature and depending on their nephew—who always was the

smart one in the family—to read to them on the rare occasions when reading was necessary, and the rest of the time living happily on the land, working with their hands—et cetera, et cetera, a là *Rebecca of Sunnybrook Farm*. As we've said over and over again in this book, in today's society if an adult doesn't read on at least a twelfth-grade level, he or she is lost amid the technology involved just in cooking dinner in the microwave or watching a movie on the VCR, and is more than likely overwhelmed by the complexity of filing a tax return, understanding a loan contract, or keeping it together from day to day on the job. He may "get by," but he is no longer one of the simple, happy folk. He is often confused, is frequently uninformed, and is almost always on the perimeter. That is no way for anyone to live.

***Everyone who is not suffering from a physiological problem (such as mental retardation) can learn to read.*** Even a person with severe dyslexia can, with the proper training, be taught to read and can learn to *like* to read. Existing programs for illiterate adults reach only about 2 to 4 percent of those in need.[3] A large portion of the other 96 to 98 percent feel that it's useless even to try to change their situation. That is probably because, through what Donald Bear calls "some educational insult" in their past, they are convinced they simply can't learn. If any of us buys into that belief, we're all sunk.

---

[3] *Ibid.*

## IF YOU CAN, OFFER
## PRACTICAL HELP

About 96,000 volunteers are now at work in the United States[4] helping adults improve their reading skills. If you feel compelled to do something, in addition to developing a healthy attitude about literacy and making it known, you can be one of those volunteers even while you're in high school. Many of Detroit's 2,500 volunteers and St. Louis's 2,300 are high school students giving one-on-one help with reading. In Florida high school and college students are involved in a tutoring program called Student Concern. In Brooklyn teenagers push carts out of libraries and onto street corners, hawking free books around the neighborhood. The Adult Literacy Initiative is given federal funds to train and pay students to teach adults to read; some of these student volunteers have even arranged to get academic credit for their work.

Of course, you can't just show up at your local library's reading program, whip out a workbook, and start tutoring a sixty-year-old mechanic. Any reputable program has a required training program for volunteers. It would also be misleading to let you think that it's going to be a real ego trip for you—something that will make you "feel good about yourself" because you're helping someone else. People who haven't learned to read by the time they're adults are usually going to have a tough

[4] Larry Mikulecky, "The Status of Literacy in Our Society," in *Teaching Reading to Older Students*, Donald Bear, ed. Reno: University of Nevada, 1989, p.3.

time learning now, and teaching can be frustrating. They may not be consistent in their attendance, may have to be reassured (by the minute!) that they're making progress, may even get angry with you because they feel they're moving interminably slowly. It's no piece of cake.

But with some training under your belt you can get to one of those special moments when the person you've struggled beside for so long suddenly gets on a roll and reads you a whole paragraph without stuttering. When you've both worked that hard, the experience can be right up there with scoring the winning touchdown.

If you want to volunteer to tutor, contact the Literacy Center, Box 81826, Lincoln, NE 68501, 1-800-228-8813. The folks there can steer you to the right place in your own community.

"If we fail," say Carl Smith and Leo Fay in their book *Getting People to Read*, "we condemn millions of the wordless to half-lives of constant bafflement, bombarded from the media by signals and messages they cannot comprehend."[5] True. But if we succeed, we help millions find satisfaction, fulfillment, and confidence, surrounded by books that provide them with beautiful language, important information, and stimulating ideas. With your help, we can succeed. You have the idea. You've picked up this book out of concern for your own parents. See what you can do for them. Then see what you can do for your world. As a rebel child of an illiterate society, you *can* make a difference.

[5] Carl Smith and Leo Fay, *Getting People to Read*. New York: Delacorte Press, 1973, p. 7.

# CHAPTER ◇ 8

# The Rest of Mark's

# Story

Mark wasn't sure what he had expected when his father started going to school to learn to read, but he was pretty sure that what happened wasn't it.

He had definitely been apprehensive about having other kids find out. Was somebody going to start acting superior and treating him like white trash? Was somebody going to suggest that he be kicked out of National Honor Society? Was somebody going to quit coming over because his dad was an illiterate now repeating third grade?

As it turned out, nobody really did any of those things. He realized early on that in a town as small as theirs, sooner or later everybody was going to know, and he decided to tell the guys himself before they picked it up from somebody else. They were all, as he put it, cool about it. Rob said, "I wish my mom would take that class. I practically have to write my own absence excuses." Brian said, "So?

What's the big deal? He's your old man. It's cool."
Steve handled it the best. He started calling Mark's
dad "the scholar" and joking around with him
whenever he came over. "Hey, why aren't you
hitting the books, guy?" "Any cute girls in your
class?" But he was supportive, always wanting to
know how it was going, always telling him to hang in
there. At first the whole issue made Mark nervous,
and he wished Steve would leave it alone. His dad
would sit back in his recliner and embarrass Mark
by actually *discussing* the subject—at length, as if
he were chatting about the baseball scores. Still, it
seemed to make his father feel good. It was as if he
were thinking that if Mark and his friends could
accept him even though he was only now tackling
the basal reader, maybe anybody could.

There were only two people in school that Mark
had a problem with—a couple who'd been going
together forever and whom everyone called "Drag-
net." Missy and Vince seemed to think that the
moral code of the entire student body was their
responsibility, and they kept their dual finger on the
pulse of everyone's problems. Nothing was sacred.
If anybody had a ripple in his life, it became
common knowledge via Vince and Missy and was
dealt with ad nauseam at cafeteria, library, and
biology lab tables for days—or until the next juicy
piece of gossip came along.

Finding out that Mark's dad was enrolled in an
adult reading class was a smorgasbord for them. The
fact was passed around with comments like, *"Poor
Mark. He must be so embarrassed."* "How could a
kid who's so smart in school have a father who can't
even *read?"* "Why go to school now? At his age he
ought to just forget it!"

Naturally, Mark got wind of it. He was bound to. Kids were coming up to him in the halls, saying, "Your old man's taking a *reading* class? Man, that must feel weird!" At first he was angry. Unlike him, they didn't have the *facts*; they didn't know what they were talking about. Besides, it was one thing for *him* to feel a certain sense of shame, but for other people to impose that on him and suggest that his dad was anything but totally together for doing what he was doing—that was something else.

But in spite of himself, the attitude and the talk caused Mark to stop and take a look at his own feelings. Was he totally proud of his dad, or did he wish he had just stayed a closet nonreader? Was he completely behind his dad, or was he still mad because he had never learned to read in the first place and was now torturing Mark with all this?

As usual, it was a little thing that answered those questions for him. About six months after his dad started classes, the family went out to dinner on a Sunday afternoon. When they were settled into the booth at the restaurant, Mark's mother picked up the menu and started her customary out-loud read-through, a practice Mark now knew had always been for his dad's benefit. But she hadn't even gotten past the first appetizer when his dad stopped her. He'd been scanning the menu himself, and now he put his hand on his wife's arm. "I'm having the roast beef," he said, "with mashed potatoes and gravy and a salad. Blue cheese dressing." And then he grinned and added, "Eight ninety-five."

Mark watched as he closed the menu and leaned back in the seat to have a look around. He was becoming more like everybody else. He was becoming able to do the little things that everyone took for granted, and it was making him a happier, more relaxed person. What was wrong with that, Mark asked himself. Between the two of them, Missy and Vince weren't half the person his dad was all by himself.

But Mark also noticed his mother as she responded in a way he'd been picking up on lately and didn't quite understand. There was an "Okay, fine," in her manner as she turned to help Debbie with the menu. Earlier that week his dad had volunteered to start helping with the bills soon; she'd sniffed and said she could handle it, and did he have a *problem* with the way she'd been doing it all these years? Another night he was reading some can labels to her while she was fixing dinner and she'd shooed him out, telling him he was in her way.

Mark didn't get it. She *said* she wanted him to go to school. She helped him with his homework, and she didn't belittle him in front of people. But at times it was almost as if she resented his changing because of the things he was learning. It made no sense.

It was actually his chemistry teacher, Mr. Morse, who helped him figure it out. About the time Missy and Vince were running Mark's story through the gossip mill, Mr. Morse asked him to drop by after school one day. He said he needed some help with the test-tube and beaker washing, but it was obvious that he really wanted to talk about what was going around and how Mark was handling it. It was the first time anybody had seemed to be aware that there was something for Mark *to* handle, and he was too grateful to play any game of, "Hey, it's cool. I'm dealing with it, no sweat."

Instead, Mark poured it out, all of it. His mixture

of pride and shame. His fear of people knowing and his anger when they knew and didn't understand. He even told Mr. Morse about his mother and her puzzling attitude.

"Life's a funny thing when you get to be an adult," Mr. Morse said to that one. "Your situation may be a pile of dog-doo, but if it's a familiar pile of dog-doo, the only pile you've ever known, you're sort of scared to change it. Of course, once you do, you usually realize it's a heck of a lot easier without the smell and the mess and the flies. Your dad's already realized that. It's harder for your mom."

Mark still didn't get it.

"She's afraid of how all this book-learning might change your dad," Mr. Morse said. "What if he doesn't need her anymore? What if he finds out when he really gets this reading business down pat that since he can pay his own bills and write his own letters, she's pretty much useless!"

Mark bridled. "He loves my mom," he protested.

"Of course, he does. But it'll take her a while to trust that he loves her because of who she is, not what she's always been able to do for him. You wait and see. They'll work it out."

After that, Mark became a regular at cleaning test tubes. Grading freshman pop quizzes. Cleaning lab stations. Anything else he could do to have an excuse to talk to Mr. Morse, who became a support group of one and was usually able to help Mark through any snag he hit. Mr. Morse seemed really interested in how Mark's dad was learning, what kind of coursework he was getting, how fast he was progressing. But more than that, he was concerned about Mark and how it affected him. He didn't always have the answers, but it was good to have somebody who would listen and didn't say things like, "What's the big thing?" Without him, Mark wasn't sure he would ever have gotten it all straight in his mind.

Mr. Morse also made it easier for Mark to convince his dad that it was okay to come to Parent-Teacher Night. In the past it had always been his mother who had done that duty, visiting his and Deb's teachers, getting the scoop on how they were doing in class. His dad, afraid of humiliation, had hardly ever darkened the door of their schools. But when Mark told his father that Mr. Morse knew about his schooling and wanted to meet him, his dad grunted—and then was standing at the front door, sport shirt on, car keys in hand, on P-T Night, ready to do his parent thing. Mark stood for what seemed like an hour stacking and restacking lab manuals while the two men chewed the fat. After that his dad was so high that they even stopped in on his history, math, and shop teachers. He passed on the English teacher, but it was a start.

A week later he did the same thing at Debbie's school. As far as Mark was concerned, the effect of his dad's change was biggest—and best—when it came to Debbie. There weren't as many arguments about homework when Dad was doing his at the same time. When she saw him chewing his pencil and breaking out into a sweat—but keeping on—she started doing the same. "I've been fighting with her since kindergarten," his mother grumbled to Mark one night while they were doing the dishes and father and daughter were bent over their books at the dining room table. "I've done everything from acting out Christopher Columbus to lining up peanuts with my nose for math lessons, and she screams the entire time. He walks in, opens a book, and she turns into a future valedictorian!" But even she looked secretly pleased.

When his father had decided to go back to school, even before his mother came back from the convalescent home, Mark had visions of his father's learning to read making their whole life better practically overnight. Those visions popped like so many suds in a bubble bath almost at once. In the first place, it was going to be a couple of years before his father was reading on a high school level and thus was on a par with adults who functioned easily in society. So it would be that long before there could be a difference in his job—a raise or a promotion or something. They might never change as a family—they might never do intellectual stuff like go to museums or study the atlas before they went on a vacation or spend evenings reading Emily Dickinson to each other (the way Missy *said* her family did). The question arose in Mark's mind more than once: would it ever make *any* difference to them?

Mr. Morse told him to look for the little things. He did, and he found them:

His father asked him about his schoolwork almost daily. Mark had never had that kind of interest taken in him beyond, "Have you gotten that homework done?" Now they were starting to discuss world issues and controversial subjects. His dad couldn't read about them in *Time* yet, but he was perusing *Reader's Digest* at a pretty good clip, and he had things to talk about that Mark could relate to. Slowly, it was improving their relationship.

His father laughed more and could take a joke without snapping everyone's head off. Maybe it was because he was more relaxed, now that he wasn't hiding something all the time. Mark and Debbie had always been somewhat afraid of him. They had looked up to him and respected him, but they'd feared him, too. Now he was human, and they were slowly becoming less scared to approach him.

In public, his father was less blustery and boastful. He didn't talk long and loud about how good a carpenter he was or how hard he worked or how much common sense he had. He didn't have to. He didn't have to try to be somebody he wasn't, or save face with himself because he felt inferior, or try to prove that you didn't have to be an intellectual to be important. He saw what he was becoming, and that was enough for him.

There was something in their house that Mark had never known was missing, but now that it was there it did make a difference. That something was *hope*.

Things could possibly get better now. You could get somewhere and have something to show for all your hard work. You could be something more in the future than you were at this very moment. You could feel that in their house, and it made the day-to-day hassles a lot easier to handle.

And it made Mark a different person. About a year after his father started school, Mark could feel that in himself. If his father could go from a second-grade to a seventh-grade reading level in twelve months, then anybody could do just about anything. Mark could go into sports medicine—and travel—and maybe do a little free-lance writing on the side. His father had proven to him that life is what you make it if you're willing to take the risks and ignore the criticism and work.

But maybe the biggest difference to Mark was that he had had a hand in it somehow—that in spite of his own shame and anger and fear he had stood behind his father, helped him sign up for the class, and just by being there convinced him that he could do it. He himself had been the difference. No matter what doubts he'd had along the way, he could be proud of that.

# Appendix I

## WHERE TO GO FOR HELP

If you've looked under every stone in your community and still can't uncover a reading program for adults, try contacting any of the following national organizations. They have personnel whose sole job is to steer you in the right direction.

ADULT BASIC EDUCATION
Regional Office Building #3
Room 5636
7th and D Streets & SW
Washington, DC 20202

LITERACY VOLUNTEERS OF AMERICA
700 East Water Street
Midtown Plaza, Room 623
Syracuse, NY 13210

LITERACY ACTION, INC.
201 Washington Street SW
Atlanta, GA 30303

NATIONAL AFFILIATION FOR LITERACY ADVANCE
101 Ostrom Street
Syracuse, NY 13210

NATIONAL LITERACY COALITION COORDINATOR
1704 Kilbourne Place NW
Washington, DC 20010

THE ALTERNATIVE SCHOOLS NETWORK
1105 West Lawrence Avenue
Chicago, IL 60604

THE PROJECT FOR ALTERNATIVE LEARNING
17 1/2 South Last Chance Gulch Mall
Helena, MN 59601

EVEN START
(This is a brand-new federally funded program; for information, contact the Chapter I reading teacher at your school.)

# Appendix II

## WOULD YOU MAKE A GOOD TUTOR?

You don't have to be a professional teacher to be the best person to teach adults who want to learn to read. Maybe the skills you already have qualify you to train for this important job. Check out this profile. If you fit it, consider seriously going to your nearest tutor training center.

### Patience

Sometimes learning seems very slow, but that's because the learner has to *gain* skills herself, not just see the tutor demonstrate his. If you have the patience to wait for the beautiful words, "Oh, I see," you have the patience to be a tutor.

### Understanding

When nonreaders come for help, they are usually burdened with social problems that they have to face without the knowledge that education gives. You can't solve their problems, but you can listen, and you can make it your business to know where to direct them if their problems are too big for them to handle alone. You also have to be able to understand when they can't concentrate on reading because they have a sick child, have just lost a job, have been evicted from their apartment. Finally, you must truly understand the problems of the reading-disabled adult and be free of critical attitudes toward him or her. Be absolutely honest with yourself. Do you respect him for trying, or do you secretly judge him for not having learned before?

## Concentration

Your main job is to teach, and your session with your student must be just that—a teaching session. You have to be able to leave your own problems behind and do everything you can do in the short time given you.

## Adaptability

Can you teach just as well if you have to move to another room? If your student's four-year-old is coloring with crayons on the floor? If your student needs pictures and demonstrations of everything instead of just words?

## Kindness

It's very difficult for an adult to admit he's having trouble doing what is expected of a six-year-old. He or she may rely on compensating behaviors, such as pretending to know what she doesn't really understand, to cover it up. If you can be gentle with those feelings, you can establish mutual trust; then those behaviors won't be necessary for the person anymore. You have to be able to figure out something to say besides "No" when a person makes a mistake.

## Enthusiasm and Encouragement

Are you able to give genuine encouragement? Can you convey a feeling of achievement over small successes? Are you able to wait for those small successes to occur before you give encouragement, or do you say everything is great? Do you have a genuine respect and regard for people who are willing to work hard to learn to read?

## Sense of Humor

Can you see the light side of most situations? Is it in you to be able to laugh at yourself and to get other people to laugh at themselves? If you can reduce tension with laughter but keep sarcasm out of the picture, you could add pleasure to someone's hard work.

## Dedication

A tutor has to realize that she can't always achieve big successes with a student, and she has to keep plugging with the small successes and short-term goals. You never know how far the ripples go from the pebble you drop in the pond. You may never know the influence you have by teaching someone. You may be teaching a potential leader. After all, Michael Faraday, Abraham Lincoln, and Harriet Tubman were all poverty-stricken, non-formally educated people. You may be teaching the parent of kids who will be saved from delinquency and the dropout league because Mom is focusing on learning. If you can dedicate yourself to looking at the growth potential, and if you can keep on working at it even though not every class session shows major improvement— you're dedicated enough to be a tutor.

## Creativity

If you decide to be a tutor, you'll be given some basic tools and simple instructions on how to use them. It will be up to you to give those tools and tricks your own personal sparkle. Can you do that?

## Perseverance

Can you hang in there in situations like these?
- The student doesn't show up for the first session.
- The student doesn't show up regularly.
- The student's progress is slower than you expected.
- The student isn't motivated.
- The student has so many personal problems that it's hard to get any teaching done.

## Commitment

If you're a person who gets fired up about a new project and then burns out after the first few days, tutoring a nonreader isn't for you. If you can make a real commitment to the job—go through the training course and teach at least one student for two one-hour periods each week for a year—you can greatly influence at least one person's life.

# Appendix III

## SAMPLE LESSON*

The following is a sample lesson and a sample written plan for a beginning reading student in an adult program. Sharing this with a parent who is afraid to try a reading class may alleviate some fears that it will be "too hard now."

* Reprinted by permission of The Literacy Volunteers of America.

# INITIAL CONSONANTS

| Action | Tutor Says | Student's Response |
|---|---|---|
| 1. Tutor writes s in manuscript, points to it.<br><br>s | This is an s. | |
| 2. | What is the name of this letter? | s |
| 3. | Listen for the sound of s at the beginning of these words—sun, sink, socks, sandwich. Do you hear the sound? | (hopefully)<br>yes |
| 4. | You say these words after me—<br>sun<br>sink<br>socks<br>sandwich<br>sail | sun<br>sink<br>socks<br>sandwich<br>sail |

| Action | Tutor Says | Student's Response |
|---|---|---|
| 5. | Which of these s words—*sun, sink, socks, sandwich, sail*—do you want for your key word to help you remember the sound of *s*? (Often a key word will mean more if the student can identify with it. When picking a key word, it is better not to use a blend such as *snake* or *tree*. It is easier for the student when you use a word with a single consonant beginning. You might suggest a key word from an experience story.) | (Student selects a word. Let's assume the word *sun* was selected.) |
| 6. Tutor writes student's key word in manuscript under s. | *Sun* is your key word to help you remember the sound of s. | |
| 7. <br><br> s <br> sun | Think of the beginning sound in *sun*. Notice how you hold your lips, tongue and teeth. Now, let out just the first sound. <br><br> (If the student, within a reasonable time, fails to make the desired response, supply it.) <br><br> /sss/ is the sound of the letter s. | /sss/ |

8.  Here are some words. Listen. Do these words
    start with the s sound:

    sausage                                      yes
    forest                                       no
    Monday                                       no
    salad                                        yes
    summer                                       yes

9.  Now, let's move this sound to the end of the
    word. Listen to the last sound in these
    words, and repeat the words:

    gas                                          gas
    kiss                                         kiss
    bass                                         bass

10. What is the last sound in these words?       /sss/

11. Tutor points to s.

    What is the name of this letter?             s

    ┌─────────────────────────────────┐
    │                                 │
    │                                 │
    │  s                              │
    │  sun                            │
    │                                 │
    └─────────────────────────────────┘

12. Tutor points to sun.

    What is your key word?                       sun

/sss/

13.

What is the sound of *s*?

14. Student writes as tutor points.

Will you write an *s* right here?

(A beginning student may need more
writing practice of individual letters,
using your manuscript letters as models.)

s

sun

s

15. Tutor prints capital *S*.

This is a capital *S*—the same name, the same
sound. You use a capital letter for a name
which begins with *S*.

sS

sun

sS

S

(If your student already writes in cursive, you
should write the *s* and *S* in cursive, too.)

NAME ___John___     DATE ___May 23___

GOALS: To read the drivers' manual and pass the written test.

| Objectives | Techniques | Material | Time | I* | Student Progress |
|---|---|---|---|---|---|
| 1. Divide 10 words from spoken vocabalary into clusters and pronounce. | Word Pattern: Multi-Syllabic | —paper, pencil, cards | 10 min. | R<br>M<br>R | |
| 2. Learn to identify and know prefixes *un* and *mis*. | Word Pattern, Comprehension, Discussion | —list of words with *un* and *mis*. | 5 min. | I | |
| 3. Learn 5 sight words- (page 3-manual) | | —list of 5 sight words. | 15 min. | I | |
| 4. Read page 2 of manual with no more than 3 errors. | Oral Reading | —manual | 10–15 min. | R | |
| 5. Identify the meanings of 3 road signs by shape. | Sight words | —Stop, yield, danger signs. | 10 min. | R | |
| 6. Read for fun. | Read silently | —News story | 5–10 min | | |

Notes:

Evaluation:

Future Plans:

# Appendix IV

## OTHER BOOKS THAT MAY INTEREST YOU

In addition to the books listed in the Bibliography, these books may be helpful to you in learning more about illiteracy, particularly if you're interested in becoming a tutor.

Colvin, Ruth. *A Way with Words.* Syracuse, NY: Literacy Volunteers of America.

———. *I Speak English.* Syracuse, NY: Literacy Volunteers of America.

Keene, Teresa. *Tips for Tutors.* Chicago: Chicago Public Library.

Lee, Doris M., and Allen, Richard V. *Learning to Read through Experience.* New York: Appleton-Century-Crofts.

Otto, Wayne, and Ford, David. *Teaching Adults to Read.* Boston: Houghton Mifflin Co.

Rauch, Sidney J., ed. *Handbook for the Volunteer Tutor.* Newark, DE: International Reading Association.

Robbins, Edward L. *Tutors Handbook.* Washington, DC: National Reading Center.

Sleisenger, Lenore. *Guidebook for the Volunteer Reading Teacher.* New York: Teachers College Press.

U.S. Department of Health, Education, and Welfare, Office of Citizen Participation. *Volunteers in Education.* Washington, DC.

# Appendix V

## FUNCTIONAL READING WORD AND PHRASE LIST FOR ADULTS*

Even though you won't be your parent's tutor, you may want to help out with this list of basic words and phrases the functionally literate adult needs to know.

| | | | |
|---|---|---|---|
| a | an | back | boat |
| able | and | bar | body |
| about | any | be | box |
| accept | apartment, | beauty | bread |
| account | apt. | because | break |
| add | application | been | breakfast |
| address | are | beer | building, |
| admit | area | before | bldg. |
| after | arm | begin | bus |
| age | army | belong | business |
| ahead | as | benefit | but |
| aid | ask | beside | butter |
| air | at | besides | buy |
| all | automobile, | best | by |
| allow | auto | better | |
| also | automatic | between | call |
| altogether | available | big | can |
| a.m. | avenue, | bill | car |
| American | ave. | birth | care |
| amount, | away | block | case |
| am't. | | board | cause |

charge

check

children

church

cigarette

city

class

clean

cleaner

clothes

coat

coffee

cold

color

come

company,
   Co.

complete

condition

continue

corner

cost

could

cream

credit

cross, crossing

daily

danger

date

day

dealer

delivery

department,
   dept.

dependent

did

dime

dinner

disability

distance

district

do

doctor,
   Dr.

dollar

done

don't

door

down

dress

drive

driver

dry

during

duty

earn

east

easy

edge

egg

electric

emergency

employ

employment

enter

equipment,
   equip.

escape

establish,
   est.

estate

estimate

etc.

evening,
   eve.

ever

every

exceed

exit

experience

express

eye

fat

feet,
   ft.

female

finance

fine

finish

fire

first

fish

floor

following

food

foot

for

former

found

free

Friday,
   Fri.

from

front

full

furnish

furniture

game

gas

gasoline

get

give

glass

go

goes

good

group

guard

had

hair

half

hand

hardware

has

have

he

head

hear

heart

heat

height,
   hgt.

help

her

here

high

him

his

home

| | | | |
|---|---|---|---|
| hospital, | lease | meeting | night, |
| hosp. | leave | member | nite |
| hot | left | men | no |
| hour, | license | metal | north |
| hr. | life | mile | not |
| house | like | military | now |
| how | limit | milk | number, |
| husband | line | minute, | no. |
| | liquor | min. | nurse |
| I | live | Miss | |
| ice | loan | modern | occupation |
| if | local | Monday, | of |
| in | long | Mon. | off |
| include | loss | money | office |
| income | low | month, | oil |
| individual | | mo. | old |
| information, | machine | monthly | on |
| info. | made | more | one |
| installment | mail | mortgage | only |
| insurance | make | most | open |
| into | male | motor | opposite |
| is | man | move | or |
| it | manager, | Mr. | order |
| | mgr. | Mrs. | other |
| join | many | much | our |
| just | mark | must | out |
| | married | my | over |
| | material | | own |
| keep | maximum | name | owner |
| kind | may | narrow | |
| kitchen | me | national | page |
| know | mean | near | paid, |
| | means | need | pd. |
| large | meat | new | paint |
| last | mechanical | next | paper |
| law | medical | nickel | park |

| | | | |
|---|---|---|---|
| part | rent | side | suit |
| pass | repair | sign | Sunday, |
| pay | residential | signal | Sun. |
| payment, | rest | signature | supply |
| pymt. | restaurant | since | system |
| period | return | single | |
| person | right | size | take |
| pick | road | slow | tavern |
| picture | roof | small | tax |
| place | room | smoke | telephone, |
| plan | | snow | tel. |
| please | safe | so | television, TV |
| p.m. | safety | social | term |
| point | said | society | than |
| police | sale | sold | that |
| present | sandwiches | some | the |
| price | satisfaction | son | their |
| private | Saturday, | south, | them |
| prohibit | Sat. | so. | there |
| prompt | save | special | these |
| promptly | saw | speed | they |
| property | say | stamp | this |
| provide | school | stand | those |
| public | security | start | thru |
| | see | state | Thursday, |
| quality | self | station | Thurs. |
| quarter | serve | stay | ticket |
| quiet | service | steel | time |
| | sex | stock | tire |
| radio | shall | stone | to |
| rate | she | stop | too |
| real | shoe | store | tool |
| reason | shop | street, | trade |
| record | should | st. | traffic |
| red | show | strike | truck |
| register | shut | such | Tuesday, |

| | | | |
|---|---|---|---|
| Tues. | vegetable | weight, | with |
| turn | vehicle | wgt. | women |
| two | | welfare | word |
| type | wait | were | work |
| | walk | west | write |
| | want | what | |
| under | was | when | |
| unite | wash | where | year, yr. |
| United States, | watch | which | yellow |
| U.S. | water | who | yes |
| up | way | wife | yet |
| upon | we | will | you |
| use | week, wk. | window | your |

\* Mitzel, M. Adele, in *Adult Education*, Winter, 1966. Reprinted by permission of The Adult Education Association of the U.S.A.

## USEFUL WORDS FOR FILLING OUT FORMS

| | |
|---|---|
| date | mailing address |
| month | present address |
| year | zip code |
| name | city |
| Mr. | state |
| Mrs. | telephone number |
| Miss | business telephone |
| first name | home telephone |
| last name | citizen |
| maiden name | citizenship status |
| middle name | birthdate |
| middle initial | date of birth |
| address | place of birth |
| street | age |
| permanent address | height |

weight
Social Security number
marital status
married
separated
divorced
widowed
single
occupation
employer
firm
place of employment
self-employed
length of service
references
in case of emergency
education
years of schooling

last school attended
degrees held
diplomas held
salary
hourly
weekly
part-time
full-time
temporary work
sex
male
female
health plan coverage
medical history
physical impairment
driver's license number
signature

# SIGNS IN CAPITALS*

A minimum list of words and phrases one should be able to read for "physical safety, social acceptability, and avoidance of embarrassment."

## General Signs

| | | |
|---|---|---|
| ADULTS ONLY | CAUTION | DENTIST |
| ANTIDOTE | CLOSED | DON'T WALK |
| | COMBUSTIBLE | DO NOT CROSS, |
| BEWARE | CONTAMINATED | USE TUNNEL |
| BEWARE OF | CONDEMNED | DO NOT CROWD |
| THE DOG | | DO NOT ENTER |
| BUS STATION | DANGER | DO NOT INHALE |
| BUS STOP | DEEP WATER | FUMES |

* Reprinted with permission of Corlett T. Wilson and the International Reading Association.

DO NOT PUSH
DO NOT REFREEZE
DO NOT SHOVE
DO NOT STAND UP
DO NOT USE NEAR HEAT
DO NOT USE NEAR OPEN FLAME
DOCTOR (DR.)
DOWN
DYNAMITE

ELEVATOR
EMERGENCY EXIT
EMPLOYEES ONLY
ENTRANCE
EXIT
EXPLOSIVES
EXTERNAL USE ONLY

FALLOUT SHELTER
FIRE ESCAPE

FIRE EXTINGUISHER
FIRST AID
FLAMMABLE
FOUND
FRAGILE

GASOLINE
GATE
GENTLEMEN

HANDLE WITH CARE
HANDS OFF

HELP
HIGH VOLTAGE

IN
INFLAMMABLE
INFORMATION
INSTRUCTIONS

KEEP AWAY
KEEP CLOSED AT ALL TIMES
KEEP OFF (THE GRASS)
KEEP OUT

LADIES
LOST
LIVE WIRES

MEN

NEXT (WINDOW GATE)
NO ADMITTANCE
NO CHECKS CASHED
NO CREDIT
NO DIVING
NO DOGS ALLOWED
NO DUMPING
NO FIRES
NO LOITERING
NO FISHING
NO HUNTING
NO MINORS
NO SMOKING
NO SPITTING
NO SWIMMING
NO TOUCHING
NO TRESPASSING
NOT FOR

INTERNAL USE
NOXIOUS
NURSE

OFFICE
OPEN
OUT
OUT OF ORDER

PEDESTRIANS PROHIBITED
POISON
POISONOUS
POLICE (STATION)
POST NO BILLS
POST OFFICE
POSTED
PRIVATE
PRIVATE PROPERTY
PULL
PUSH

SAFETY FIRST
SHALLOW WATER
SHELTER
SMOKING PROHIBITED
STEP DOWN (UP)

TAXI STAND
TERMS CASH
THIN ICE
THIS END UP
THIS SIDE UP

UP
USE IN OPEN AIR

USE OTHER        VIOLATORS WILL   WARNING
   DOOR            BE PROSECUTED WATCH YOUR
USE BEFORE                          STEP
   (DATE)        WALK              WET PAINT
                 WANTED            WOMEN


## Car Related Signs

ALL CARS          END                  ONLY
   (TRUCKS)          CONSTRUCTION   LEFT TURN ONLY
   STOP           ENTRANCE          LEFT TURN O.K.
ASK ATTENDANT     EXIT ONLY         LOADING ZONE
   FOR KEY        EXIT SPEED 30     LOOK
                                    LOOK OUT FOR
BEWARE OF         FALLING ROCKS        THE CARS
   CROSS WINDS    FLOODED              (TRUCKS)
BRIDGE OUT        FLOODS WHEN       LISTEN
BUS ONLY             RAINING
                  FOUR WAY STOP     M.P.H.
CAUTION           FREEWAY           MECHANIC ON
CONSTRUCTION                           DUTY
   ZONE           GARAGE            MEN WORKING
CURVE             GATE              MERGE LEFT
                  GO SLOW              (RIGHT)
DANGEROUS                           MERGING
   CURVE          HOSPITAL ZONE        TRAFFIC
DEAD END                            MILITARY
DEER (CATTLE)     INSPECTION           RESERVATION
   CROSSING          STATION
DETOUR
DIM LIGHTS        JUNCTION          NEXT
DIP                  101 A          NO PARKING
DO NOT BLOCK                        NO LEFT TURN
   WALK           KEEP TO THE       NO PASSING
   (DRIVEWAY)        LEFT (RIGHT)   NO RIGHT TURN
DO NOT ENTER                        NO RIGHT TURN
DRIFTING SAND     LANE ENDS            ON RED LIGHT
DRIVE SLOW        LAST CHANCE       NO SMOKING
                     FOR GAS           AREA
EMERGENCY         LEFT LANE MUST    NO STANDING
   VEHICLES          TURN LEFT      NO STOPPING
   ONLY           LEFT TURN ON      NO TURNS
END 45               THIS SIGNAL    NO "U" TURN

NOT A THROUGH STREET

ONE WAY

DO NOT ENTER

ONE WAY STREET

PAVEMENT ENDS

PLAYGROUND

PROCEED AT YOUR OWN RISK

PRIVATE ROAD

PUT ON CHAINS

R.R. RAILROAD CROSSING

REST ROOMS

RESUME SPEED

RIGHT LANE MUST TURN RIGHT

RIGHT TURN ONLY

ROAD CLOSED

ROAD ENDS

SCHOOL STOP

SCHOOL ZONE

SLIDE AREA

SLIPPERY WHEN WET (FROSTY)

SLOW DOWN

SLOWER TRAFFIC KEEP RIGHT

SPEED CHECKED BY RADAR

STEEP GRADE

STOP

STOP AHEAD

STOP FOR PEDESTRIANS

STOP WHEN OCCUPIED

STOP MOTOR

THIS LANE MAY TURN LEFT

THIS ROAD PATROLLED BY AIRCRAFT

THREE WAY LIGHT

TURN OFF

TURN OFF ½ MILE (¼ MILE)

TRAFFIC CIRCLE

TRUCK ROUTE

UNLOADING ZONE

USE LOW GEAR

WATCH FOR FLAGMAN

WATCH FOR LOW FLYING AIRCRAFT

WINDING ROAD

YIELD

YIELD RIGHT OF WAY

# Bibliography

Biggs, Shirley, and Bruder, Mary N. "Adult Memories of Early Reading Experiences," in *Teaching Reading to Older Students*, Donald Bear, ed. Reno: University of Nevada, 1989.

Chisman, Forrest P. *Jump Start: Final Report of the Project on Adult Literacy*. Southport Institute for Policy Analysis, January 1989.

Clarke, Louise. *Can't Read, Can't Write, Can't Talk Too Good Either*. New York: Walker and Company, 1973.

Colvin, Ruth J., and Root, Jane H. *Tutor*. Syracuse, NY: Literacy Volunteers of America, 1984.

Costa, Marie. *Adult Literacy/Illiteracy in the United States*. Santa Barbara: ABC-Clio, Inc., 1988.

*Encyclopedia of Associations*, 24th ed., 1990.

Greene, Bob. "ABC's of Courage." *Reader's Digest*, Vol. 133, August 1988, pp. 126–128.

Hampshire, Susan. *Susan's Story*. New York: St. Martin's Press, 1982.

Hunter, Carman St. John, and Harman, Davis. *Adult Illiteracy in the United States*. New York: McGraw-Hill, 1979.

Jones, Edward B, *Reading Instruction for the Adult Illiterate*. Chicago: American Library Association, 1981.

Kirsch, Irwin S., and Jungeblut, Ann. *Literacy: Profiles of America's Young Adults*. Princeton: Educational Testing Service, 1986.

Kozol, Jonathan. *Illiterate America*. New York: Doubleday, 1985.

———. *Prisoners of Silence*. New York: Continuum Publishing Corporation, 1980.

Lin, Lisa. "Illiteracy in America." *Seventeen*, Vol. 47, April 1988, p. 98.

Logan, Carmela H. "Integrating ESL/ABE and Mainstream Teacher Training," in *Teaching Reading to Older Students*, Donald Bear, ed. Reno: University of Nevada, 1989.

Mickelson, Carolyn. "Unreadable Pain." *Seventeen*, Vol. 47, April 1988, p.97.

Mikulecky, Larry. "The Status of Literacy in Our Society." *Teaching Reading to Older Students*, Donald Bear, ed. Reno: University of Nevada, 1989.

National Advisory Council on Adult Education, *Illiteracy in America*. Washington, D.C.: U.S. Government Printing Office.

Neilsen, Jerry O. "Societal Consequences of Adult Illiteracy," in *Teaching Reading to Older Students*, Donald Bear, ed. Reno: University of Nevada, 1989.

Nickse, Ruth S.; Speicher, AnnMarie; Buchek, Pamela A. "An Intergenerational Adult Literacy Project: A Family Intervention/Prevention Model." *Teaching Reading to Older Students*, Donald Bear, ed. Reno: University of Nevada, 1989.

Palmer, Julia Reed. *Read for Your Life*. Metuchen, NJ: Scarecrow Press, 1974.

Park, Rosemarie J. "Three Approaches to Improving Literacy Levels." *Teaching Reading to Older Students*, Donald Bear, ed. Reno: University of Nevada, 1989.

Safran, Claire. "Illiteracy: Read All About It." *Woman's Day*, October 1, 1986, pp.86–87 and 119.

Smith, Carl B., and Fay, Leo C. *Getting People to Read*. New York: Delacorte Press, 1973.

Stedmen, Lawrence, and Kaestle, Carl. "Literacy and Reading Performance in the United States from 1880 to the Present," in *Teaching Reading to Older Students*, Donald Bear, ed. Reno: University of Nevada, 1989.

# Index